Secrets of Top Money
Extra Income

Secrets of Top Money
Extra Income

Edith L. Johnson

Parker Publishing Company, Inc.
West Nyack, N. Y.

Library of Congress Cataloging in Publication Data

Johnson, Edith Line,
   Secrets of top money extra income.

   Includes index.
   1. Self-employed. 2. Supplementary employment.
3. Part-time employment. I. Title.
HD8036.J63   658.1'141   75-23357
ISBN 0-13-798090-6

How This Book Can Help You Achieve Top Extra Income

Today many people are looking for additonal income to handle the constantly rising cost of living. For several years I have worked successfully at improving my own income situation. Moving into a better-paying position is one way to increase the money flow, but has its limitations. You can go only so far, and you are always at the mercy of those above you.

In recent years I have concentrated on developing and producing "extra income" money. This is a rewarding activity not only financially but also in self-satisfaction. It offers you the hope of an even brighter future ahead, since extra income activities frequently become highly profitable full-time businesses.

This book will help you find the kind of extra income activity that is right for you and show you how you can turn this activity into big profits by working only a few hours a week.

The book is designed specifically for those who want to improve their present financial position. It will motivate you to take the first step along the way to certain success. It shows you how to discover your own money-earning potential and to put it to work for your special benefit. You will learn numerous ways to turn your everyday activities into money-earning operations with little extra effort on your part. Hundreds of successful part-time businesses, producing top money income, are described.

You don't even need to step out of your own home if you don't want to, nor do you need to sacrifice large amounts of time.

Everything is here to show you, not only how to earn good money in your free time, but how to have fun doing it.

There are many workable formulas for success, but mine is geared specifically to success in second-income ventures. It shows you how to turn every minute of your free time into money with proven examples of others who have put it to work.

You will become acquainted with a housewife who started decorating cakes for her friends and neighbors, and soon found herself operating a cake decorating and wedding business which now brings in over $50,000 a year.

A man in his late sixties, who had never made more than a modest income from his job, used his knowledge of real estate to turn small investments into big profits. He is now worth over a quarter of a million dollars.

Learn how a handyman who advertised that "We do anything," developed his service into $75 to $100 a day business, and how a successful leasing business that started in a spare room of the house has grown into one of the largest leasing operations in the state.

Discover the simple formula which makes it possible for you to put in extra hours of work without sacrificing any valuable time. You can actually take on extra income activities after your regular workday and still find plenty of time for leisure.

An untrained auto mechanic with natural ability started repairing cars for his acquaintances. Later he leased a service station and suddenly discovered he had a gold mine in his sideline business. Word-of-mouth advertising was his best business producer: soon he had all the business he could handle. He worked out a system where, with little cost, he could keep his service station customers personally serviced without having to devote his full attention to them.

This book gives you numerous examples of unusual businesses that began as part-time ventures. It gives you detailed information on how to get the necessary capital, secure customers and run the business efficiently and easily.

My result-producing step-by-step instructions take you all the way from a low-capital beginning to a top money-making venture that could become one of the best "rags to riches" success stories yet to be printed.

Edith L. Johnson

Contents

2. HOW TO UNCOVER UNDEVELOPED OPPORTUNITIES   (cont.)

3. NEEDED CAPITAL AND LITTLE KNOWN METHODS FOR ACQUIRING IT 41

4. SUPPLYING PART-TIME SERVICES FOR BUSINESSES 55

4. SUPPLYING PART-TIME SERVICES FOR BUSINESSES (cont.)

5. TURNING YOUR HOBBIES INTO A PROFITABLE SECOND INCOME · · · · · · · · · · · · · · · · · · · 69

6. INNOVATIVE WAYS TO FOOD-MAKING PROFITS · · · · · · · 83

8. SECOND-INCOME OPPORTUNITIES FOR THE
    VERSATILE WORKER   (cont.)

9. SECRETS OF BIG MONEY IN PRODUCT MANUFACTURING . .   122

11. TIPS ON UNUSUAL PROFIT-MAKING
OPPORTUNITIES IN TEACHING   (cont.)

12. OFFERING UNUSUAL YET MUCH NEEDED SERVICES 166

14. BUILDING TOWARD A FULL-TIME BUSINESS
        OR RETIREMENT   (cont.)

1

Revealing Secrets That Enhance Your Earning Ability

Whether we are wealthy or poor, most of us have the desire to acquire more money. This urge to build a fortune, or at least attain a more comfortable income, exists and persists at most levels of earning power.

Some, however, have greater success at fulfilling this desire than others. Frequently it is the one who starts at the lowest rung on the ladder who rises to the greatest financial height. Obviously, then, success does not need to be the privilege of a few. It can be available to anyone who will take time to discover the secrets and apply the effort necessary to put them to work.

M.D. Pruitt, owner of a large furniture store, began his career selling mattresses from his garage. He started his business with $64, his wife's first pay check. With this he bought a two-wheel trailer and two mattresses, and ran a classified ad in the local newspaper. One hour after opening his store he had his first sale. Twenty-two years later his business was grossing $9 million with a 100,000 square foot retail building and 126,000 square foot warehouse.

He has built his business on sound principles, selling only brand name merchandise at the lowest possible price. He never has discount sales, and allows no high-pressure sales tactics in his store.

Dr. Jaye Marchant was a high school dropout scrubbing floors when she determined to own a sorority pin and a diamond ring like those owned by her boss's wife.

The daughter of itinerant fruit laborers, she worked at many different jobs and barely scraped out a living, but today she is worth $4 million. The details of some of her business ventures are described later in this chapter.

You will find many of the basic fundamentals behind these successes in this chapter, and the chapters which follow will give you numerous true-life examples of how they were accomplished.

Read carefully, making sure you understand every word. Once you have read the material and absorbed it thoroughly, the next and most important step is to apply this material to your own life. Decide which approach is most suited to your capabilities and start putting its principles to work immediately.

SETTING YOUR GOALS FOR THAT EXTRA INCOME

Setting a goal is one factor that can never be overlooked if you are to expect any level of success. You can't head for a destination until you know where it is. Setting a goal is much the same as selecting a destination. Until you know where you are going you won't know what road to take or, perhaps even more important, which one not to take.

You can always recognize a Sunday driver. He drives slowly and aimlessly. The man who knows where he is going and who has a purpose in getting there will travel as fast as the law will allow.

You, too, without some sort of definite goal, will be nothing more than a Sunday driver.

Pearl J. was 65, struggling along on Social Security, until she read *Think and Grow Rich* by Napoleon Hill which stressed not only having a goal but also writing it down along with the date on which you want to achieve it.

Pearl decided she wanted to earn an additional $300 a month starting the end of that month. She lived in a central location, had a nice big back yard and was home all day, so she put an ad in the paper which read: "Take your preschool child to grandma's house." Before long she had so much business that she had to turn children away—all this *after* she set a goal.

Some people create a goal by getting into debt. One sales manager urges his salesmen to go on a spending spree when they are in a slump. The indebtedness gives them something definite to aim for.

Dr. Marchant uses this technique. She has a particularly strong sense of responsibility and uses it to force herself to produce. Her abilities expand to meet her needs. She has, in fact, earned $4 million in the past 3½ years by acquiring a $20 million indebtedness. The most important milestone of her career, she says, was when her debt load increased to a point she could no longer afford to work as a secretary.

What do you really want that you haven't bought because you

can't afford it? A new carpet? New car? New house? Add them all up. Contact the salesmen who sell these things. Compute the down payment and exactly how much you'll need to meet the monthly payments. Now you have a definite goal.

Whatever your method, be sure you do have that goal. Decide now what you want to accomplish, when you want it done and how you are going to do it. Make a list of every possible way you feel you might accomplish the goal and select the method that best suits your particular situation.

ORGANIZING YOUR FREE TIME FOR PROFIT

Start organizing your time now and you will discover the amount of free time you can find will be in direct proportion to how badly you want what you have set as your goal.

To organize your time you should make a list of everything you need to accomplish in order of importance. First in order is your ultimate goal to be accomplished in six months, a year—whenever you decide. You will then need a list that spells out what you will accomplish the first month. After that you can get down to the finer details as you list what you must accomplish the first week.

Now, on a day-to-day basis, you can put the plan into action by making a detailed list each morning of exactly what you must handle on that specific day. As each action is completed, cross it off the list. It is almost like making an outline for a book manuscript. When you know exactly what you must do in order of importance, the actual follow-through will be much simpler.

In the process of organizing your time, it may be necessary for you to eliminate some frills and unnecessary activities from your routine. This won't be too difficult to do if your goal is important. You will discover, as time goes on, that you do have time to indulge in enough leisure-time activities to adequately satisfy your needs.

HOW TO MAKE MONEY AND ENJOY DOING IT

Many a leisure-time hobby has become a booming business because someone discovered they had something that other people wanted.

Ben J. always enjoyed writing and decided many years ago that this was the way for him to make a living. When Ben made that decision he began looking for every opportunity to improve his writing ability. While earning a living from other means, he wrote whenever the opportunity arose.

I have known several artists who worked at other jobs while they painted on the side. They used every possible means of displaying their art, even in sidewalk shows. I know one artist who exhibits arts and crafts in shopping centers. He displays his art with others, and makes several thousand dollars on his paintings at every show. By doing what he enjoys he is making top money.

Making big money doesn't mean you have to become a drudge, sacrificing all the pleasures of life. You are far more likely to succeed if you discover a way to put a hobby you enjoy to work for you.

Take a look at your own hobbies first when making plans for a business. Decide what you really like to do, then find a way to present it to others.

Promote your particular ability, whether it is making some item or performing a special service. In this book you will find many examples of people who have done this successfully. As you read, apply the principles of their actions to your own situation.

The two necessary steps are: Discovering what you like to do best and promoting your ability along these lines.

NEARLY $5,000 EARNED IN THREE WEEKS—PAINTING WINDOWS

Jaye Marchant, the former dropout mentioned earlier in this chapter, was always drawing and painting when she was young. She discovered a way to put this pastime to work for her many years later.

At age 35 she went back to college to study law and decided to paint Christmas designs on store windows to earn some of the extra cash she needed. By the time she received her doctorate she had become involved in real estate, but her window painting served her well in those early years.

In a three-week period she made $200 the first year and $4,800 in the same time the second year, continuing in school all the time. She started selling to the stores in mid-November and began actual painting around Thanksgiving.

Some of her Christmas customers approached her to do their windows for holidays throughout the year. She worked out a package deal for them for eight holidays. She estimated that her earnings in this kind of setup would have brought her approximately $20,000 a year.

Her biggest expense was paint. It took about $100 worth of paint to do $5,000 worth of windows.

She used a couple of good sabeline brushes for outlines and house paint brushes for filling them in. She also got a variety from a one-inch brush to a calcimine brush for large snow areas.

A black and a yellow crayon or marking pencil is necessary for sketching outlines, and a razor scraper is needed for cleaning up the drips after the paint is dry. A small squeeze bottle can be used for adding water to thin the paint, which can be mixed in half a dozen small icebox-type plastic containers. You'll also want a plastic dropcloth for the trunk of your car. (Dr. Marchant said a Volkswagen works well for such work, because you can drive it right to the front of the window, lift the hood and be all set to paint.)

You will need a bucket and a couple of plastic gallon jugs for water to clean brushes between windows.

Meat paper is good if you want to make patterns, but you won't need this if you do the work freehand directly on the window. If you aren't good at freehand art, simply make patterns as Jaye Marchant did in the beginning. Tape the pattern on the inside of the window, looking out, then go outside and paint as if you were painting in a coloring book.

Ideas for designs are easy to find in children's Christmas books, Christmas cards or magazines. Jaye Marchant charged from $15 to $30 a window and has done some large car dealers' windows for as much as $150. She averaged $1 per running foot with a $15 minimum.

THE FIVE MOST IMPORTANT CONSIDERATIONS

Whatever business you choose for your second income money, there are several important factors to be considered before you make the big step. Careful advance planning always makes for better business operations.

Here are five considerations that will assure proper planning:

1. What can I do? You will want to take a good look at all your capabilities and decide what you do best and enjoy doing most. When evaluating your abilities, don't eliminate anything as too minor or insignificant. List *everything* you feel you can do with a fair amount of skill and then decide which fits the following considerations best.

2. Is there a demand for this? This you can determine largely from observation. Inquire among the people you know and can become acquainted with through businesses or organizations about the marketability of your service or product. Wherever possible, try it out on a small scale and see for yourself how it sells. As long as you are starting this as a second income you can afford to try it out cautiously in the beginning. You should do this as thoroughly as possible before you invest a great deal of your time or money.

3. What is the income potential from this? You will need to figure as nearly as possible what your cost per sale will be for your product or service. Take the cost of the material you must use; then compute the time it will take you to complete it. Charge double that amount for your profit. When you decide how much time you can give to the operation you will have a fair estimate of its future financial potential.

4. How long will it take to reach this potential? This should not be too difficult to estimate when you have worked out the details of Step 3. Once you know how much time you can give to the operation and what your profit is for that time, it should be a matter of simple addition to determine when you can hope to reach your goals.

5. How can I maintain myself while reaching that potential? This will probably depend largely on how much work you can handle "after hours" and for how long. You may want to take a look, also, at the possibility of turning this into a full-time operation somewhere along the line *before* it has reached its top potential.

All these considerations must be handled by each prospective business owner in his own way, but they should be carefully answered before the actual business operation is undertaken.

PERFORMING SERVICES YOU HAVE WANTED FOR YOURSELF

Probably one of the most certain ways to know you have a business that is needed is to offer a service you have wanted but have been unable to secure.

An embarrassing situation—when a businessman's secretary failed to pay a bill owed to a friend for a three-month period—

caused the businessman to start a computerized service for busy professionals and business executives. The service takes care of their utilities and other personal bills that usually don't fall within a monthly schedule. It prepares checks for signature and gets them ready for mailing.

What are some of the services you have been wanting for yourself but couldn't find? One of them might be something you can offer at a profit to yourself.

FINDING OPPORTUNITIES CLOSE TO HOME

The first step toward discovering what is wanted and needed in your own neighborhood is getting acquainted with the people living there.

One of the best places to start is in your neighborhood laundromat. Many people congregate there for fairly long periods of time, providing ample opportunity to talk to them and discover their needs.

Local organizations such as PTA and churches offer equally good opportunities to get acquainted with people and uncover possibilities for services you could render.

You should certainly contact businesses in your neighborhood, inquiring not only about their needs, but also observing what they need.

Terry J. turned her observations into a $15,000-a-year part-time job. She gets lists of customers from service stations with the dates when they will need lubrication jobs, and reminds the customers when it's time to get the job done. The service stations pay her a percentage on each job.

TEN WAYS TO DISCOVER OPPORTUNITIES ALL AROUND YOU

1. *Income Opportunities,* a monthly publication, has specific instructions and how-to information for numerous business opportunities. There are several other specialized opportunity publications with this type of information. Study these at your local library or purchase a copy in a nearby drugstore or newsstand.

2. Many special-interest magazines describe income opportunities that fit their particular publication.

3. Read the want ads in your local paper, especially the

miscellaneous columns. One couple put many deals together by simply matching the "Wanted to Buys" with the "Wanted to Sells."

4. Don't forget the "Help Wanted" columns—especially sales positions. Nothing gets done without a sale. Look for something you really believe in that fits the needs or desires of your group of acquaintances. You don't have to sell for only one company. Get familiar with several products or services and their salesmen. These people often pay for leads.

5. The bulletin boards of local laundromats have a wealth of information on local needs. Grocery stores often have similar bulletin boards where people post requests for services or products. You can also use this source to inform others of what you have to offer.

6. See what others have done. You don't have to use a new idea: there is nothing wrong repeating success. Actually, it is often better to start with something already tried and proven.

7. Examine your own special talents. What can you do better than someone else? It might be some kind of artwork, cooking, carpentry work, or special repair. Capitalize on your abilities.

8. Special requirements at holidays and birthdays offer rich opportunities. Especially around holidays, a lot of people are too busy to perform all the little tasks so important to special seasons. They'll pay others to do them. Are you good at cooking special holiday treats? One lady, who always sent her own family a Christmas box filled with homemade goodies, extended this gesture to her friends and co-workers. Soon she had more orders than she could fill.

In another case, several women who liked giving parties made a successful business of setting up birthday parties for children of busy parents.

9. Look for things that need to be done around your neighborhood. A vacant lot might have provoked a complaint to the health department. Find the owner and offer to clean it up.

Fay L. had no particular artistic talent but was a neat painter. She watched for signs that were still clear but faded and made excellent money by simply refreshing the paint at a reasonable rate.

You might see a spot where a favorite flower from your garden would be an asset. Stop and offer to plant them, using your own cuttings.

10. Read "how-to" books in your local library on specialized subjects that appeal to you.

Mac C. bought a book on shoeing horses, then bought a barrel of hoofs from a slaughter house on which to practice. By the end of the barrel he had learned the trade well enough to earn $10 to $15 for each shoeing job, and he learned it without hurting a horse.

FUTURE POTENTIAL OF YOUR SPARE TIME BUSINESS

In this book you will read about numerous examples of people who turned small part-time ventures started in their home or garage into highly productive businesses. Many of them are millionaires today. Study these examples carefully, following the instructions outlined throughout the book, and you too should be able to develop a spare time operation that can become a top-paying business.

An important fact to remember is that anything worth doing is worth doing well. The success of your venture depends entirely upon how you handle it right from the beginning. Plan each step carefully and follow that plan through to a successful operation.

ASSESSING YOUR OWN ABILITIES AND PAST EXPERIENCES

Take an inventory of yourself and your abilities: are you a good cook, a capable fix-it man or auto mechanic, an expert on the English language, an artist, a neat housekeeper or yard man? Examine every area without eliminating anything as too menial or unimportant.

Gerald L. developed a knack for short-order cooking when he worked for a drive-in restaurant. He is now the prosperous owner of several night clubs serving food and drinks. He makes about $12,000 a year in cash and owns assets worth a quarter of a million dollars.

Mark J. had a special talent for cutting men's hair. He came to town with only $4 in his pocket and set up a barber shop on a back street. Very soon he became the favorite barber of most of the prominent leaders at city hall. He made about $50 a day.

Many famous recipes have been discovered in private kitchens by housewives who had never marketed a commercial product before.

If you are performing a service or making a product which has received considerable commendation from your family or friends, perhaps you should look into the possibilities of turning this into a profitable venture.

It might be well, also, to recall some of the things you have done in the past and long since forgotten: maybe something you did in school was highly successful or a job you held some years back required special skills. Perhaps you forgot all about something you used to make.

Edna B. used to do some unique things with old furniture when her parents were too poor to buy anything new for their home. She painted baby items on nursery furniture, flowers and attractive symbols on other items and matched odd pieces together to make a set. Later she revived this talent, painting decorations on furniture for a furniture store. She used a special paint and technique on some of their items, giving the furniture the appearance of polished leather. Her pay was the additional amount the furniture sold for after she refinished it. She made about $100 a week doing this.

So take a look at yourself and discover some assets you never before realized you possessed.

FITTING YOUR ABILITIES TO THE NEEDS

You can't put a square peg in a round hole, nor can you put a profitable talent to use where that particular ability isn't needed. So once you have found within yourself the hidden abilities you have to offer, the next thing you must do is ascertain where this talent is most needed and wanted.

One of the quickest ways to discover this is through a classified ad. In this way you can quickly discover what need there is for your product or service, at a small expense.

You can also display your product or the description of your service in public places by paying a certain percentage on what you receive from such displays, or make your offering known through friends and acquaintances.

It is often possible, also, to draw upon related experience in an operation of a somewhat different nature. I did this when I got my first public relations job. I had no actual experience in public relations work or in putting together a company magazine, which was what the job called for. When my prospective employer asked me if I had ever put out a house organ, I didn't want to say "No," because I wanted that job. Instead I described all the things I had done which had some similarity to this type of work. I told him about my experience as editor of two weekly newspapers and about some of my freelance writing and mentioned my work in a print shop and in the layout and printing of a weekly press club bulletin. After telling him all the positive aspects of my experience, I admitted I had never put out a company publication. I got that job which was the beginning of a satisfying public relations career for me. You can frequently fit your abilities to the job or business at hand even though the experience is not identical.

WHERE TO GET ALL THE FACTS YOU NEED FOR SUCCESS

One of the first places to look for information which will help you succeed is in the success stories of others. You should study these thoroughly, especially those that relate to your particular type of business venture in some way.

Your public library is a source of almost any specialized information you need for a business you wish to undertake. In the library, or through a bookstore if necessary, you should find every book that tells you how best to perform the service or make the product you have in mind.

You will find many sound principles in the success stories of others who have started small and become big in this book. Many of these will tell you what you need to know in order to make your own business successful.

The Small Business Administration has many pamphlets on almost any kind of business venture you might consider. These give detailed information on how to start and develop a business operation.

You can write to the Superintendent of Documents, U.S. Government Printing Office, Washington, D.C. and ask for a list of titles on pamphlets, books and booklets about job opportunities and business careers. You can order those which are best suited to your situation from a selection of over 30,000 titles.

HOW TO TAKE THE MOST SUCCESSFUL APPROACH

It is never advisable to plunge into anything of importance without careful planning. This is particularly true in the case of a new business venture. The best possible approach to a successful business venture lies in targeting your goals and laying out specific procedures for their fulfillment.

When you are ready to begin, make yourself and your service or product known and establish a contact with others who can help you.

Be sure you know what is needed and wanted—then produce it.

Handle any situations that interfere with the best interests of your business as they occur making sure that none of these will occur again.

Promote your business well, be careful of your expenditures in the beginning and deliver what you have agreed to produce.

If you follow these rules, your enterprise should be off to a good start which will continue to prosper as a successful business venture.

FINDING ALL THE TIME YOU NEED WITHOUT STRAIN

If you organize your time carefully as outlined in this chapter, you will discover that you have a great deal more time than you ever imagined.

I have discovered my own ability to produce has increased beyond belief. Through planning and organization I have been able to handle a 40-hour-week public relations job, write a daily newspaper column and take a course two nights a week with ease.

One simple factor that makes all the difference is the completion of every cycle of action you undertake. When you lay out these specific programs of action every day as outlined under the heading "Organizing Your Free Time for Profit," be sure you complete every action started each day.

Incomplete actions and unfulfilled goals can cause utter confusion and extreme fatigue. But if you plan your action well and complete what you start out to do, you will be able to accomplish twice as much work as you have before—with half the effort.

An excellent source of information on this subject is in the book *Problems of Work* by L. Ron Hubbard.

THREE SECRETS TO ACQUIRING HIGHER LIVING STANDARDS

There are three simple rules that, when followed closely, will assure any business venture of success and its owner of a much higher standard of living. They are:

Know where you want to go;

Know how to get there;

Then make the best of the situation when you arrive.

2

How to Uncover Undeveloped Opportunities

You don't need to dig a hole in the ground to find buried treasure, but you might do well to dig deeply within your mind or experiences. A careful search within yourself could very possibly uncover some unique ways to make all the extra money you have been seeking.

Much of the wealth of this country has been made by people who did something with an untried or undeveloped idea.

Bob Schulte developed a new and better cleaner for vinyl car tops because he had so much trouble trying to clean the vinyl top on his own car. His repeated efforts to find a cleaner that really worked convinced him of the need for this product. He wasn't a chemist but his daughter and son-in-law understood chemistry. Schulte and his son-in-law worked with some chemists to develop a formula for a cleaner that would do the job effectively. Schulte then developed a marketing plan to reach 30 million potential customers with vinyl car tops.

He wasn't stopped by lack of finances or the fact that banks often don't make loans for good ideas. Instead he raised his initial $45,000 from individual investors who had the choice of converting to stock when the company was in operation or of merely offering their money as a loan with interest. All but two of the original investors converted to stock. A year later stock ownership grew to $150,000 with plans to expand into cleaners for other types of vinyl. Bob's personal investment in the beginning was between $500 and $1,000.

Be alert to everything around you—your own needs and desires and those of others. There is an idea lurking somewhere in your experience. Find it and use it.

FIVE WAYS TO DISCOVER NEEDED SERVICES

Often when someone gets a big break the general public believes that the successful person was in the right place at the right time. This is only partially true: there are many other factors that enter into the situation.

Here are five workable suggestions for discovering needed services in the right places:

1. Attend mass-sale public market places. Auctions, flea markets, swap-and-shops and any special sales markets are excellent places to find out about needed services.

Friends of mine have used the services of David P., who attends auctions, sales markets and the like wearing a shirt inscribed with the word "Hauling." He goes there with his truck and picks up all the work he can handle hauling merchandise to the homes of the buyers.

Arnold R., who repairs antique furniture, develops all the business he wants at these special sale places.

The important thing is to be on the lookout for what is needed and make your services known to those who might want them.

2. Door-to-door solicitations. People are looking for all types of services in their homes and around their yards. A visit to every house in the neighborhood in which you wish to work can uncover many needs.

If you are timid about asking for work you might employ a unique method I learned from a friend. Art L. was handy around the house, so he had cards printed saying:

SSH
(Save Sweet Husbands)
STOP NAGGING
I'll do those undone chores for you.
What do you need?

All he had to do then was present the card at each residence and wait for a response. He got all kinds of odd jobs, from repairing water faucets to house painting. He made from $65 to $70 a day. This is something that could be done both by men and women. You can specify the types of chores you are most capable of doing if you wish.

On the other hand, if you want to offer any and all services, you can work with others and set up a business where you do some of the work and act as an employment service for others who might do what you can't handle.

3. Office solicitation. This can be handled in a way similar to door-to-door house solicitation. Instead of looking for a regular salaried job, you'll be seeking customers on a regular basis for services not easily handled by regular personnel. It might be delivery services, telephone solicitations for the firm, address typing, office cleanup, special photography, handwritten notes to customers, or research work. You'll have to discover extra needs regular staffs cannot handle easily.

4. Yellow Pages. You should study the yellow pages of your telephone directory with the thoroughness of a research analyst. That section of your telephone book is full of so many ideas for services that its pages could keep you busy every day of your life.

Study those businesses listed and described, then decide which businesses might have needs which fit your abilities. Start a campaign to get their business. This can be handled by phone, in person, by letter or with a combination of all three.

Jim R., a young man in his late teens, used a letter campaign effectively. He sent letters to every business that he felt had the slightest possible need for his services, and he received offers that an experienced business executive would welcome. He did, in fact, become a successful executive in a short period of time.

5. Publicize your services in a different way. Several years ago when I wanted a particular job for which there was a great deal of competition, I made sure that my written application would be noticed. I answered a blind ad and followed its instructions specifically, sending a two-page resumé as requested. The position was in publicity and advertising: any ingenuity showing my creativity along those lines would be good promotion for me. I took some stationery with a light desert wash on it—just enough to make it stand out a bit, but not enough to seem overdone. Then I typed in the center of the page, "Yesterday I sent you a two-page resumé as requested. Today I am reminding you of my telephone number.

I then typed out my number across the center of the page.

Out of more than fifty applicants I was one of the few to get an interview and later was offered the job.

Some time ago *Reader's Digest* published a quip which read:

Looks like a lady
Thinks like a man
And works like a dog.

Mae C., a secretary, used this ad when she was looking for a job. She added her special qualifications at the bottom and got over 30 responses.

Running just any ad isn't enough. Think of a different approach. This particular ad is best suited to women, but men can think of an original angle, I am sure. Make the ad different and effective. Don't sacrifice solid information for cleverness, but think of a different way to give the factual information about yourself.

SUPPLYING SERVICES FOR EVERY NEED

One individual can't supply services for every need, but each individual wanting to develop a business by providing a service should know there are many needed services waiting to be done. There are opportunities available to those willing and able to seek them out. If you prefer to discover needed services and turn the actual work over to others, you may be able to supply services for all the needs you uncover.

There are many people who have service capabilities but lack the ability to promote themselves. If you have the ability to research opportunities and promote services, you might consider representing people with service capabilities, such as freelance artists, freelance public relations people, or business management consultants. This can be very profitable business if you make yourself knowledgeable about the services offered and represent only qualified and reliable people. It can be done with a very minimal investment by selling services on a percentage basis. You can avoid the expense of hiring people to do these jobs for you if you merely secure the jobs for them for a fee.

This differs from the usual employment service because you would go out and find opportunities before selling your clients' services. The commission would be ongoing on a monthly basis like that of a literary or theatrical agent.

There are many people who would be willing to pay for this service. I have paid an ongoing commission for some special writing projects secured for me, and know management consultants, public relations specialists and other professionals who would also gladly do this.

WHERE TO FIND NEW OPPORTUNITIES

Small or newly opened businesses often provide new sources of opportunities for services, since many of them cannot afford full-time employees for all their needs.

Watch the newspapers, particularly the financial pages, for stories about new businesses you can visit in person. You may be able to secure a number of these small firms as clients, offering them a variety of services.

Ernest B., a certified public accountant, set up a business of this kind in a rapidly growing western city, drawing on his past experience with numerous business accounts. He offered a diversified service to businesses and used "diversified" as part of his firm name.

He offers all sorts of personal and business services from estate planning and management to accounting, record keeping and income tax preparation. It cost him approximately $1,500 to start his business, which now earns an annual income of $30,000 to $40,000.

This approach could be used by many other services—nonprofessional as well as professional.

Another successful business grew out of the discovery that doctor's offices are not usually equipped to handle account management with the personal touch it requires.

Ralph S. set up a computerized service which specialized in physicians' accounts. Individuals in his organization talk personally and courteously with patients who have complaints or questions. His firm emphasizes the need to maintain good relations between doctor and patient without sacrificing business efficiency.

Hal D. made a boot jack from three horseshoes which he welded together so that the smaller one caught the boot heel when a person stepped onto the larger ones. He got discarded horseshoes free and sold his products wholesale for $5 apiece. He made about $100 a week in his spare time.

Finding a need in a specialized field such as this can open the door to a ready-made business for you with almost certain immediate success.

PRODUCTS YOU CAN SELL AT A PROFIT

There are endless numbers of products which you can make and sell. The most important consideration is the profit you can realize: some products produce considerably more than others.

Luxury merchandise such as gift items, jewelry and novelties frequently sell for a much higher markup than other items. Products that have the biggest markup are those unique items that look expensive but are not costly to produce. Rare or difficult-to-find merchandise also brings a higher percentage of profit.

Some products may be expensive to produce, but their margin of profit is high enough that the original investment in the product is well worth it.

Walter S., a consultant for fish-breeding water areas, conceived the idea of making and servicing fish tanks for doctors' offices and other businesses. Some of these sold for as much as $3,000. He also received additional income from servicing the tanks.

It is good merchandising, especially in the field of luxury items, to have one or more products among those you market that warrant a higher than 100 percent markup.

COLLECTORS' ITEMS THAT ARE IN DEMAND

Scarce items, especially antiques, are always in demand. The price people are willing to pay is based largely on how rare the item is.

Dealing in collectors' items requires expertise because a thorough knowledge of values, rarity and age is necessary. While this is not a good business for the novice, ability can be acquired if you have the interest and persistence to explore and study. If you are interested, reputable antique dealers can tell you how to learn the profession .

Auctions offer an excellent source for rare items. John R. finds much of the old glass which he repairs and restores at auctions. He has always had an interest in antiques and finally narrowed his interest to stained glass after purchasing a large collection of old church windows from an elderly couple. After his first purchase he began collecting from other areas. He learned how to repair and restore the glass himself. Soon he was able to sell his restoration service to two large dealers. Individual collectors who later heard about him through word-of-mouth advertising began commissioning him to restore their glass.

His first commission was from an attorney who passed the word on to other attorneys and friends until John's private business has expanded almost more than he can handle.

He started with a $50 window and a $5 soldering gun. John's sideline is only limited by the amount of time and effort given to his work.

There are many other ways in which collecting can prove profitable. In collecting figurines as a hobby Jan B. discovered she had a rare item in her collection. Wanting to look for more rare items after that, she went to the library and got all the books she could find on the subject. She found more rare items in junk yards, at Goodwill and in swap-and-shop stores, buying most of them for very little. Finally she decided to sell some of her collection. She purchased more items with her profits and started placing her merchandise on consignment in antique shops. She makes from $10,000 to $12,000 a year this way.

DIRECT SALES APPROACH TO A BETTER INCOME

A good salesman with the right product or service can always earn top money regardless of the economic situation. Mark G. was a brush salesman. He was so successful in this field that he formed his own brush company. His investment was minimal: about $500 for rental space in a small building and brushes for five sample cases.

He contracted with a brush manufacturer to supply him with brushes as he sold the merchandise. He gradually increased his sales force and when he retired in his late forties he was making $50,000 a year.

Ralph P. learned some professional skills as a client in an antipoverty program. Later he discovered his ability and interest in sales work. Today he has an $18,000 a year sales job with a pharmaceutical company.

Direct sales offer most of the advantages of a business of your own with no financing problems. It has great potential for the person with this kind of ability. If you need further training in this field there are many sales seminars, sales institutes and specialized magazines for salesmen. If sales work interests you, study these publications and investigate some of the specialized training available. The job opportunities are plentiful. Check magazine and newspaper advertisements and discover the opportunity best suited to you.

WHOLESALING MERCHANDISE FOR EXPANDED MARKETING

Wholesaling your merchandise will offer a much wider scope for sales and, while the profit is smaller per item, the volume of sales can more than compensate for this.

Many businesses choose wholesaling instead of retailing because of the volume and lack of complication. Retailing requires much more paper work and licenses that aren't necessary for wholesaling.

Some successful retail businesses have expanded their sales areas by wholesaling on the side. I did this several years ago, when I owned a small gift shop, in handling several wholesale jewelry and gift lines for accounts throughout the state. In that case it was a supplement to the main business, but the wholesale business grew to a point where it was as profitable as the retail shop.

Wholesaling doesn't require the inventory necessary for retailing. In fact, it can be done in many cases without inventory. Sales can be made entirely from sample lines. This cuts into your profit again, but it is often better to start this way and go into stocked merchandise later when the products have proved themselves.

One big advantage to wholesaling over retailing is that you are not limited to one location and one area of customers. Your territory for sales is as large as you want to make it. If one area proves unprofitable you can always move to more productive ground.

PART-TIME MAIL ORDER OPERATION
BECOMES BIG MONEY EARNER

Thomas L. Hall writes special self-help reports and sells by mail order from Tokyo, Japan. His reports are on such subjects as beauty, health, oriental reducing diets, part-time home businesses and other self-improvement subjects.

He says he never writes more than four hours a day because his creativity wanes if he goes beyond that point. When he has completed his research and written a report, his next step is to write a sales letter which he sends to mailing lists in the United States and elsewhere.

The initial cost of supplies is small. It includes envelopes, letterheads, reply envelopes and forms and special advertising inserts in quantities of 1,000. To this he adds the cost of labelling, inserting, sorting, tying and delivering to the post office. The total cost is less than $200. Most of your mailing costs and printing expense can be paid after you actually start getting orders.

Other costs will depend on your method of advertising the report. If sales letters are sent to rented mailing lists the charge for these lists can raise the cost considerably. The least expensive route to follow is to place a small classified ad in a national magazine or newspaper that has wide circulation. Your sales letter can then be mailed to those who answer the ad asking for information.

Hall received $500,000 worth of orders for one report in three days. The secret to success in this field is a good report on a subject of general interest and a top quality sales letter.

WHERE TO GET NEW IDEAS FOR BETTER MERCHANDISING

One of the best ways to get valuable suggestions for better merchandising is to talk to a person who is doing it successfully. This isn't difficult to do: most are happy to give pointers and helpful hints to others who are getting started.

Reading business success stories in the local newspaper is one way to learn about prosperous businesses. A talk with the financial page editor might also produce some good leads.

Classes in specialized fields of business are often held in community colleges and universities. Check the schools in your area for classes or seminars on merchandising.

You can do a concentrated study of your own by visiting some of the most successful merchandise businesses in your community and noting their methods.

Make good use of your public library. If you aren't sure where to look for the information you seek on merchandising, ask the reference librarian for help.

When you receive your list of titles from the Superintendent of Documents, U.S. Government Printing Office, Washington, D.C., check it for anything on merchandising. If you don't find what you are seeking, write the Washington office and ask where you can get this type of information.

GETTING MANAGEMENT GUIDANCE TO INSURE YOUR SUCCESS

The Small Business Administration of the federal government directs all its attention toward helping the small businessman or woman. It has a special service in management guidance conducted by SCORE (Service Corps of Retired Executives). SCORE is made up of retired business professional volunteers who have been recruited by the SBA to provide free management services to small businesses. Most SBA offices have a staff member in charge of SCORE who assigns the various consultants to businesses within their particular realm of knowledge.

Some universities and community colleges have special class projects that help the small businessman. You might visit the business school of the university nearest you and see if there is a possibility of their assigning your business as a project for credit to one or more class members.

Banks, particularly, will assign a young executive trainee to a business that needs help. You might want to explore this as a possibility in your own community.

The rather expensive cost of a paid management consultant can be valuable to you and save money in the long run—*if* you choose the right consultant. The best way to discover the right one is to check with other businesses who have gone this route.

MONEY-EARNING GOALS AND HOW TO SET THEM

The amount of money you make on your second-income venture depends largely on your attitude. If you think you are limited in what you can earn, you most certainly will be. On the other hand, if you KNOW you can earn big money, you can. It is up to you to set the amount you want to attain, and then follow the necessary procedures of good business practice to make it happen.

Napoleon Hill and others suggest writing out your goal and placing it where you can see it every day. This is an excellent idea—one that I have used successfully.

Thomas L. Hall sent me a photograph of a large number of

report orders he received in one day, and suggested I put it in a prominent place where I could see it every day. This I did, reminding myself daily as I looked at that picture that I was selling that many orders in one day myself.

I have also written down the specific amount of cash that I wished to earn, kept the figure where I could see it every day and found my own money-making potential increased steadily from that point on.

It is equally satisfactory to just put it there mentally. I did this in connection with extra money I needed to handle a newly acquired financial obligation. This time I merely decided that I would find a pleasant way to save money and that I would enjoy the challenge. Later, when I found myself in this exact position—saving money and living better than ever, thoroughly enjoying the whole thing—I had forgotten my earlier decision. A friend had to remind me of the day I had put it all there, knowing it would happen.

So set yourself a definite goal and know that you will have it; then take the necessary steps to insure its fulfillment.

EARNING THOSE EXTRA DOLLARS WITH VERY LITTLE EFFORT

All you have to do if you find yourself feeling overburdened with additional work activity is think of all the things you want that this extra money will provide. If you think about the good it will give you, you won't have time to think about the work effort itself.

Most important—choose a second-income business in a field you enjoy.

Joe Acuff had tinkered with cars most of his life while he held down a government job as an education specialist. Finally he decided to give all his time to car repair and started his own business with Gulf Oil Company in one of their service stations.

He works longer hours doing more physical labor than he ever did on the government job, but he is one of the happiest men I've seen. He is doing what he likes to do. His initial investment was $3,000, and his business brings in as much as $1,800 a month. He has built a good business with steady customers because he provides good service with a smile.

Whatever you do to make that extra money, you will find yourself bringing in the money and expending very little effort in the process if you enjoy what you are doing. Make whatever you do fun and it will never seem like work.

3

Needed Capital and Little Known Methods for Acquiring It

New ideas, no matter how valid they may be, are seldom acceptable as security for a conventional loan. This makes it essential for many small businesses to acquire money through more conventional means.

There are numerous success stories of businesses that started on a shoestring. It is possible to start a business with not much more than a "prayer and a song" even today. It is more difficult than it was some years ago, but still possible with the proper know-how.

The advantage of starting a second-income business is that you can start on a smaller scale while you are still earning your living from another source. This means you can sometimes begin with less money and take a little longer to build a sizeable business.

Whether you start large or small, it can become difficult to find the necessary financing. Contrary to common belief this is the case with big business as well as with the little man. Sometimes it is much more difficult for the big operator to secure the financing he needs than it is for the small businessman.

There is a great deal of available information on financing that appears to be common knowledge but is, in fact, unknown to many business people.

This chapter has much of this information. It is unknown in many business circles only because no one researched it adequately.

Undoubtedly some of what you read here will not be new to you, but I would rather include the obvious with the less obvious so the information will fit the needs of all or most of you.

STARTING A BUSINESS WITH SMALL INVESTMENT

There are many ways to start a business with little or no capital—businesses which can easily expand to million-dollar operations. The person who has another means of livelihood while developing his business has many advantages because he isn't under financial pressure while the business grows.

Service businesses provide some of the best opportunities to start with small investments, but the small operator is not limited to this type of business. Many product-oriented businesses have been started with very little investment simply by beginning with a smaller amount of stock or using a little ingenuity in purchasing.

George P. went into the component fabrication business with $500 invested in a second-hand welder. He and a partner bought a piece of weather-worn equipment that they put in such good shape that it could do the job of a new $25,000 machine. They now have a company worth half a million dollars because they used a little ingenuity to make do with what they had.

Alice J., a former secretary, began a highly successful service in her home with no investment at all. Opening the yellow pages of the telephone directory, she called businesses to see what jobs they had available, and offered to run ads for their job opportunities free in a weekly publication. Alice's specialty was finding part-time jobs for students.

She succeeded in getting a printer to run her job opportunities newspaper at his own expense on inexpensive paper, then sold the publication through schools, rehabilitation and skills training centers and stores catering to young people. It was so successful she was soon charging these firms for their job opportunity ads, and the paper became a daily, with clear profits of $600 to $800 a month.

There are many advantages to starting with a small amount of capital: the biggest one is that the gamble is much less. Lack of funds also necessitates more economy—a sound business philosophy for a new operation.

SECRETS OF SUCCESSFUL FINANCING

The use of OPM (Other People's Money) is a valid and profitable way to start a business and is sometimes more advisable than using your own savings. The advantage is that you have more buying power, which usually means more return on your money.

There are many situations in the field of second-income opportunities where this principle is not valid except to a limited degree because the early investment returns are not certain enough. The important thing is to know the difference and to borrow in the correct amount.

For the small business it is often better not to borrow too heavily in the beginning. There is a tendency to overextend yourself if you start with too much capital; it is amazing how much you can economize when you have to. Often the need to economize stimulates the urgency to work a little harder.

Earl K., who is in property management, is an excellent example of this. He had enough money to handle heavy monthly payments so he rented an office for $385 a month. His other monthly expenses were $125 for the telephone, $175 for furniture, $300 for Yellow Pages advertising, and $30 for a water cooler. He soon found himself spending more and more time in the office waiting for telephone calls or client visits, and less and less time working in the field.

Earl soon took inventory of the situation and realized that his business was going down instead of up. He gave up the office and started working out of his home. His financial belt-tightening necessitated more concentration on his work.

He no longer has an office that "needs him," and is able to give all his time to his clients and their business interests. Since that change his business has increased constantly and consistently. When he had an office he earned from $10,000 to $12,000 a year; he now earns from $50,000 to $60,000.

So the real secret to successfully financing your second-income business is the ability to judge how much you really need, being willing to start small if necessary and build as you go.

Some persons work better under financial stress. Securing a large loan gives such a person the incentive to produce to the fullest extent. The responsibility such a person feels for paying back the loan necessitates and usually results in a highly profitable business operation. This works only in the hands of a conscientious and responsible person who *knows* the loan must be repaid.

Which type are you? Either approach can work. It is just a matter of picking the method that best suits your temperament and business.

The secret of acquiring the financing you need, once you've made this decision, is confidence in yourself, combined with the ability to sell yourself and your product or service. Seek out the lender best suited to your needs; then ask with confidence. When you approach any lender don't be defensive and compromising. Go there knowing he needs you more than you need him—because he does.

Later in this chapter you will find detailed information on the various loan sources.

HOW TO APPLY FOR AND GET BANK LOANS

The business of lending money is a vital part of any bank's operation; banks are eager to lend wherever possible. If you can prove to them you are a reasonable risk they will, more often than not, stretch a point where possible to grant your loan request.

Before applying, make yourself as aware as possible of all the factors that enter into the loan officer's decision and be prepared to tailor your request to conform with these factors.

Be ready to give him detailed information about your background to assure the bank official of your financial reliability. If you can show evidence of established credit you have won the first battle. Your past record of paying off debts will have a great deal to do with the loan officer's decision. For this reason the person who buys on credit is often better off than someone who always pays cash, since the latter has never established a credit rating—there are no records to show that he always pays cash. It is good to buy some things on credit if for no other reason than to establish your credit rating.

Be specific about the amount of money you need. Any indication of vagueness raises a question as to your ability to handle money. Know exactly how much you need and state the amount without hesitation.

Give a detailed account of what use you are going to make of the money and how you will pay it back.

To get a business loan you should have an established business even if that business is producing nothing. It is difficult to get a business loan before you have some semblance of an operation, even if it is only printed stationery, business cards, an operating address and a telephone number.

Many new business operations have to secure personal loans before they can start a business. A personal loan is not as desirable because it is more costly, especially if you can get a business loan through the Small Business Administration instead. It can, however, get you off the hook in the beginning.

If you have established a good credit record or you have assets to use as collateral, a personal loan is not too difficult to secure. If not, you might have to go the route of securing a co-signer. This may not be easy to do because the co-signer must take responsibility for paying off the loan if you default. But it can be done: where there's a will there's a way.

Albert R. and Gordon C. started what is now a million-dollar transfer company with $1,000 secured through co-signed loans. Each of them borrowed $500 from a different bank in the same town, co-signing for each other. This little trick might not work for you, but if your intent is strong enough you, too, will find a way.

FIVE WAYS TO SECURE PRIVATE MONEY

Loans from institutions are not the only means of acquiring money to start your business. There are many other equally satisfactory and more available avenues in certain situations.

Private loan sources will always be accessible to the man or woman who has a legitimate business program to offer, for many people want to get their fingers in the pie without the work of doing the baking.

Here are five ways to secure private money:

1. Offer future stock to individuals. In Chapter 2 I mentioned Bob Schulte, who raised $45,000 for his special product through friends and acquaintances.

Schulte approached the banks first and was advised to seek capital through private lenders. Since he had no manufactured product or operating business to provide security to the lender, he had only himself and his own integrity to offer.

Schulte put together an extensive portfolio that described in detail his background, experience and reliability over the years. It was a fully documented report of his business and personal history which gave clear evidence of his dependability and his capacity to operate a successful business. Along with this he discussed what his product was capable of doing and gave evidence of why his business should succeed.

The proof of his own integrity and the soundness of his business plan enabled Schulte to secure sufficient private investment to start his business. Each investor had the option of converting his money into stock or giving the money as a loan with interest. This is an excellent way to raise adequate money to start a rather large operation.

2. Advertise for money. Run a small classified ad under "Business Opportunities" and another under "Personals" in your local paper or in the nearest metropolitan newspaper. In this simple, inexpensive way, you will discover people who are eager to earn better-than-average interest on their money. If you can offer a fairly high rate of interest you should get a sizeable number of answers. Many people are willing to gamble when the stakes are high enough. You can afford the higher rate of interest if you are reasonably sure your business will pay off in a relatively short period of time.

3. Pay a commission. Find an aggressive and able salesman to whom you can pay a commission for every loan he or she secures for you in his or her area. Finders fees on small amounts of money are usually four to five percent and two percent for larger loans. You will have to provide a solid plan to present so he or she has something worth selling. The plan should show reasonable security, relatively low risk and money strength to insure loan payments. Short-term loans for three to five years are the easiest to sell.

4. Syndicate a limited partnership. With this approach you take on the responsibility of being a general partner in finding people with investment money for starting capital for your business. The standard plan for this type of investment program provides that the general partner retain (with only his time and expertise invested) interest equal to 15 percent or more. The limited partners then each hold undivided interest comprising the other 85 percent. Some might have 10 percent, others 25 percent, etc., to a total of 85 percent. The only loss these investors can possibly incur is what they have invested. They are not liable for any big company losses or setbacks.

5. Sell your excess assets. Most people have some excess material possessions that could be sold with very little sacrifice involved. Check your closets, garage and even the other parts of your house and yard for things you don't need to keep; then hold a carport or garage sale. You may be amazed at how much money you can take in from a sale of this kind.

A few years ago I raised $700 by placing items of every kind and description in my carport— furniture, kitchen utensils, equipment, dishes, glassware, clothing, even used pencils, paper clips and other odd bits. My carport was like Grand Central Station for two days, but it was worth it.

Another time, when my husband was still living, there was a period when we were spending beyond our income every month, dipping into reserve funds. To economize we traded houses and moved within walking distance of my husband's job, enabling us to get along with one car.

The money from the car sale was only one small part of our financial gain in this transaction. We saved enough on gas, oil and general wear and tear on the car every day to not only stay within our income but also to save about $200 a month.

What do you own that you could manage without? It might be the answer to financing a new business venture for you.

GOVERNMENT SOURCES FOR NEEDED CAPITAL

The small businessman who cannot get a bank loan, has no assets and has explored every other institutional or private source of money, quite often can get a loan through the federal government.

The Small Business Administration will take risks which the banks feel they cannot chance, sometimes securing a loan for you from the very bank that turned you down. This government agency is geared to lending money to small businesses where financing is not available through any other means. If your business fits the conditions of eligibility for an SBA loan, you can get 80 percent of your needs with the bank carrying a portion of it. The SBA loan limit for a single project is $350,000. There are a number of requirements for an SBA loan, but it is the one loan agency where the small businesses with no collateral at all have an advantage over big operations. If you have been unsuccessful in acquiring financing from all the usual sources, I would suggest you visit the SBA office nearest you to see if you qualify for a loan.

Other sources of government financing are the Small Business Investment Companies which are supervised and licensed by the Small Business Administration (SBA). An SBIC will make a five to twenty-year loan with competitive interest rates subject to state and SBA rules. Most of the SBIC's in operation were formed as second-income sources for groups of businessmen. There should be one in or near your community. To find an SBIC in your locality check the "Money to Invest" columns of your local newspaper.

Another source of government lending is MESBIC—Minority

Enterprise Small Business Investment Company—directed toward businesses owned and operated by minorities. If you are a minority person or have minority partners in your organization it might benefit you to check into MESBIC. You can get a list of office locations at your nearest SBA office.

PITFALLS TO AVOID IN BORROWING MONEY

One of the most serious pitfalls new business operators fall into is overextending themselves in the beginning. Even if you have a credit rating which allows you to borrow freely, don't overdo it in the early stages. Borrow only enough to be sure that you don't fall short of the operating costs you need to get started. In most cases it is better to start slowly and build your own financing as you develop the business.

Eagerness to get the money and get started can sometimes lead to borrowing money at unreasonable interest rates. Avoid this wherever possible because excessive interest can be an unnecessary burden. There are always places to find money at the right interest rate if you have a business with good potential and take the necessary time to seek out funds.

HOW TO GET THE BEST POSSIBLE TAX ADVANTAGES

There is a saying that what you don't know can't hurt you, but exactly the opposite is true as far as taxes are concerned. The more you can learn about tax laws and how they apply to you and your business the better off you will be. Lack of knowledge in this field can really hurt in a most sensitive spot—the pocketbook.

The first thing any wise business person will do is study tax laws thoroughly. You should also read the financial pages of your newspaper and every publication that gives you up-to-date information for tax news. I am strongly in favor of paying a qualified tax man to handle business taxes, but this does not eliminate the necessity of knowing about the subject yourself. For your own protection, you should be capable of checking the tax man's work as it relates to your specific situation. A thorough and up-to-date knowledge of tax laws—which change from time to time—will make it easier for you to direct your business activities toward the fullest tax advantage.

The Internal Revenue Service puts out two publications which will make you more knowledgeable of tax rules—*Tax Guide For Small Business* and *Your Federal Income Tax.*

The IRS also publishes free information on individual benefits such as depreciation, investment credit, business and individual deductions and many others.

Visit the IRS in your vicinity and secure a list of their publications or write to the U.S. Government Printing Office, Washington, D.C. 20402.

Once you understand the laws thoroughly you can look for some of the areas in which you can reduce your taxes, sometimes getting a refund of several hundred dollars. Jack G. had to pay additional taxes every year until he learned more about tax laws. Now he gets $700 or $800 refunds every year.

As your business expands you may find yourself involved in several projects. Some companies operate these related projects under sole proprietorships and deduct the various business expenses separately. Many businesses benefit from the tax advantages of multiple projects. Combine your own knowledge with that of a reliable and capable tax consultant. If both are of the best quality the combination is unbeatable.

HOW TO HANDLE LARGE INVESTMENT OPPORTUNITIES

As mentioned earlier, the large investor risks business failure to a much greater degree than the small businessman who starts on a lesser scale and works up. Consequently the large investor must know what he is doing every step of the way. No one who cannot afford to take a risk should become involved in large investment opportunities, but there would be very few millionaires in the world today if some people had not been willing to take this risk.

Large investment opportunities do not necessarily mean you must have extensive funds on hand, for more big businesses are financed on OPM than are not. The secret of success here is in the ability to lay out a proper plan, purchase when the price is right, and put the money into something that will pay its own way—something that will start bringing in returns almost immediately.

FOUR WAYS TO FINANCE THESE BIG INVESTMENTS

Institutional lenders. These lending institutions are interested in making loans to businesses that are solvent and growing operations.

Many second-income businesses start small but rather rapidly become big business operations. When heavy financing becomes necessary, these institutions may welcome your business.

Among such institutional lenders are banks, foundations, insurance companies, pension funds and credit unions. A management consultant, bank official or Small Business Administration consultant can advise you as to where to apply.

Stock offerings. Going public is, as a rule, a means of raising funds for a business that is already showing a profit, with some exceptions to the rule. It involves considerable time and expense, but has many advantages. Consider its pros and cons if you are in a position of possible acceptance for registration with the Securities and Exchange Commission. There are less complicated ways to involve outsiders in your business by means of stock offerings. For instance, you can sell a portion of your business to one individual who will receive a return on his money as the business pays off, either in a lump sum or on a percentage basis. You can also offer stock to a few people—twenty or less. This is sometimes popular among people with common interests, but must be offered only to people in the same state where your business is operated.

Another approach is to issue stock worth a maximum of $300,000 under Regulation A. You aren't required to give a great deal of information to the SEC in this type of stock issuance, and the money can be used for payroll, payment of previous debts, plant construction or anything which applies to your business. For more information on this write to the United States Securities Commission, Washington, D.C. asking for their booklet, *Regulation A. General Exemption.*

Leasing. There are advantages and disadvantages to leasing as a means of financing, but it does offer a satisfactory method for many sizeable business operations. You can lease equipment, freeing your capital for other purposes, or you can lease buildings or furniture and smaller items.

One common method of successfully generating cash is the sale and leaseback approach of selling your property through newspaper advertising or other means and arranging to have the buyer lease the property back to you for a specific time. In this transaction you must insist on outright cash—which your buyer can obtain through a bank or other lending institution—for the purchase. This method not only gives you the immediate cash you need for your business but it also saves you maintenance expense and has many tax advantages.

Venture capital. This is a source of money for many small businesses, new and established alike. Funds are available through venture capital firms for as much as $2 million or more. These are usually available as long-term loans, sometimes for as much as twenty years. Venture capital firms frequently offer management and counseling as well as money.

Venture capitalists provide an excellent source of funds for the new business, product or service that has potential. These firms and individuals are willing to take risks and participate in speculative projects where chances for sizeable gain appear evident.

THE RIGHT TIME FOR PUBLIC STOCK OFFERINGS

Most public stock offerings take place only when the business is operating satisfactorily, indicating profit and progress. The stock offerings are made at such a time to raise funds for expansion. With a second-income business this is usually when the business has outgrown its part-time stage, making financing necessary to bring it into full-time operation.

There are exceptions to this notion, especially in the sale of private or limited stock. There are cases, too, like that of Bob Schulte, where money is raised through individuals with the understanding it can be converted to stock when the company has progressed to the point of issuing it.

There is also a time when you can go back to the public for additional money after your first stock issuance. If your company has shown a profit by paying stockholders dividends, and you can give evidence of even larger returns with additional funds, you should be able to sell more stock. Your best bet here is to give the original stockholders the first chance to purchase new issues.

It is possible sometimes to issue stock again even though there have been no profits or dividends if you can provide convincing evidence that additional funds will correct this situation.

SECRETS TO DISCOVERING MONEY SOURCES OFTEN OVERLOOKED

If your desire to start a business is strong and your confidence in the potential of the business is firm, lack of money should never get in your way. There are money sources all around you: all you need to do is find the right one.

Many that I will mention are seemingly obvious, but are nevertheless frequently overlooked.

Industrial giants. General Electric, Standard Oil, American Can and Emerson Electric are just a few of the industrial giants that give seed money to specially selected new business operations. Many of these companies which make provisions for venture capital prefer not to make it publicly known, fearing a deluge of requests. This is an area you should investigate if you have something that you think will be worth the consideration of one of these big businesses.

Insurance loans. Insurance companies sometimes furnish money to a new business at interest below the going rates. Insurance loans are frequently but not always for small amounts. This can be a means of obtaining substantial sums.

Commercial Finance Companies. These companies operate like a standard finance company but don't charge the same exorbitant interest rates. They lend money on accounts receivable, inventory, plant machinery and equipment. They will provide funds on time sales paper and handle equipment leasing, real estate and export-import financing.

Personal property. You can often finance property through a mortgage on your home. Additional money can sometimes be acquired this way even when you already have a mortgage.

Discounted mortgages. If you are holding a mortgage on property you have sold, you can get a lump sum for that mortgage by discounting its total worth. If you feel your business gains will surpass the loss on the mortgage, this is a quick, sure way to acquire the cash you need.

SIX WAYS TO CUT EXPENSES WHILE DEVELOPING A BUSINESS

1. Set up space in your home or garage to cut down on rental costs.

2. Buy used or junked equipment, furniture or fixtures and put them in working order yourself.

3. Use an answering service instead of employing a full-time telephone receptionist.

4. Buy materials in small quantities and use profits to purchase more. Build your stock gradually as the business grows.

5. Do it yourself and work longer hours, if necessary, before hiring extra help.

6. Rent equipment instead of buying it. This not only cuts down on investment, but it also gives you a tax advantage.

Alton S. saved $2,000 in his first year in the auto repair business by applying these principles.

BUILDING A BUSINESS WITH OTHERS' MONEY

You don't need to wait until you have accumulated years of savings to start your business. You can start it today with Other People's Money and make money in a short space of time as Jaye Marchant did. Many other people, too, have started their businesses on OPM.

If you study the techniques outlined in this chapter and demonstrated throughout the book by example, you too can soon enjoy the magic of OPM. You can forget jobs with limited salaries and make the sky your limit.

MANAGEMENT SECRETS THAT SAVE YOU MONEY

Good management encompasses a lot of things: your money outlay, your time, your selectivity in what you buy and your expertise in what you are doing.

Take inventory of yourself in all these areas and if you are lacking in any, remember that there are management people available to help you. The secret of success is learning what you don't know, and doing what you do know.

HOW AND WHEN TO REINVEST ALONG THE WAY

There are two entirely different indications of when it is wise to reinvest in your business.

One is when the business is doing well, showing a profit and ready for an expansion program which additional funds can handle.

The other indication is when the business is not showing a profit, but it is clearly evident the condition can be corrected with more money.

In the first case you may be able to reinvest by returning your profits to the business. In the second instance you will probably need to secure another loan. The validity of your judgment of the need will be tested when you seek that loan.

Listen carefully to the reasoning if you are refused and make valid corrections—but don't give up. Remember that there are many places to go when you need additional funds. If you know your plan is solid and your chances of success good, borrow and reinvest.

4

Supplying Part-Time Services for Businesses

There are literally hundreds of small business operations that need a variety of clerical services but can't pay full-time employees to do them. This is a fertile field for the person who has the skill to fill these needs.

It is possible to earn from $3 to $10 an hour for any of the specialized types of services, particularly those that require professional expertise. The secret is that a small businessman can afford to pay you the higher hourly rate for a few hours a week more easily than he could ever pay a full-time salaried person for the same service. This enables you to handle several accounts while working only a few hours a week.

There are also numerous opportunities to perform part-time services that require no particular skill. The only skill needed is that of seeing a need where it exists and recognizing your ability to fill it.

The best area of all for developing untapped sources for clients is through your own creative imagination and observation. A number of small businesses aren't aware of some of their own needs. If you can show these businesses how a specific service will increase their profits, many will be interested.

You can uncover some of these needed services by studying other more progressive small businesses. Discover what they have that others don't; then offer to supply one or more of these services to those who need them.

Once you have determined, in your own mind, that there are potential customers for your service—before you make any bids for business—set up your own operating quarters and organize your approach.

SETTING UP WORK SPACE AT HOME

One secret of success is to operate—at least at first—from your home where the cost is minimal. A secretarial or clerical service lends itself to this very easily.

There are many ways to do this even when your living quarters are small. Ideally, there are two important considerations—privacy and space—but sometimes both of these have to be compromised.

I have set up business at home under a variety of circumstances and saved anywhere from $200 to $500 a month, enjoying the luxury of a separate room for my office a couple of times. In both instances I was able to turn one bedroom over to the business.

In another situation it was necessary to set up office space in a one-bedroom apartment. Here I set aside a portion of the bedroom for a desk, typewriter stand, typewriter and chair, and placed the filing cabinets in the closet.

One period of my writing activity was handled in a tiny apartment using a section of the kitchen for files and one end of our dining table for typing. It was a little crowded since I had to use this table for my mixer too, but my husband and I managed without too much difficulty.

Sometimes a garage or a porch area can be made into an office. This might mean some additional expense if you need to install heating or wiring, but it is still less expensive than renting space away from home.

In some instances you may need to partition off one end of a room to make space. Whatever your situation, you can find the needed room under almost any circumstance when necessary, and have fun meeting the challenge.

MINIMAL EQUIPMENT NEEDED

Very little equipment is necessary for this type of service. The amount will depend on the extent of service you plan to offer. Much of what is needed can be used or makeshift. At most you will need a good used typewriter with stand and chair, a desk or table space, filing space, record books and some supplies.

The desk, files and typwriter stand can all be makeshift. I have used a table for a desk and fruit crates for files. You will probably need to improve your files in short order, however, so I would suggest buying the cardboard file drawers in the beginning. They are much less expensive than metal file drawers and will serve the purpose well until your business is bigger. You can save from $50 to $100 this way.

If you don't plan to offer typing services, then your equipment needs will be considerably reduced. You may need only table space, record books, paper, pencil, pens and other supplies.

This is a business you can start on very little investment with proper management. Clerical work—in your home or in a business office—can often lead to bigger and better things. It can teach you a great deal about the kinds of businesses with which you deal. This knowledge, properly used, can become a gold mine.

CLERK TYPIST BECOMES MANAGEMENT CONSULTANT

Marguerite T. worked in the New York office of a management association as a clerk typist. Part of her job was to sort out and catalogue magazines as they came in.

To familarize herself with the business, she added, on her own initiative, the job of dusting the books in the firm's private library. Whenever a title interested her particularly, she would take the book from the shelf and read it during her break and lunch periods. The more Marguerite read, the more knowledgeable she became of the business. Soon she was made the association's executive secretary. In this position many association members discussed concerns with her. Frequently, in answer to a problem, she would cite something from one of these books.

As time went on her knowledge of management became more and more evident to all who worked with her, and she was called to Washington, D.C. for consultation on some of the association's business. This recognition gave her the confidence necessary to open her own consulting service and, in a reasonably short period of time, she became management consultant for some of the largest companies in this country, making from $1,000 to $2,000 a month. The secret to her success was her constant search for more knowledge and ability to absorb it.

TEMPORARY JOBS THAT PAY WELL

You may not want to commit yourself to steady working time, in which case it would not be wise to set up a home service for businesses.

If you want to work a few days or a few weeks at a time, taking a vacation now and then, the secret to good pay, job variety and fewer working days is the temporary job market. There are several employment agencies in cities throughout the country that specialize in temporary job placement, and they usually secure a high hourly rate for those they place. These jobs are generally for office workers—secretaries, stenographers, bookkeepers and typists.

OLDER WORKER FINDS ANSWER IN TEMPORARY JOB MARKET

Marjorie G. had great difficulty finding work because she was older than most clerical workers and was extremely conscious of this fact. She was an excellent bookkeeper, but couldn't find a decent job until she tried one of the temporary placement bureaus. She then got an excellent bookkeeping job which lasted several weeks and brought her $4.75 an hour. Her earnings permitted her to stop working for a few weeks at the end of this job. She felt secure, also, in the fact that she could easily, with the help of this agency, find another good paying temporary position whenever she wanted it.

If there aren't any employment agencies for temporary help in your community, advertise for temporary work in your local newspaper or contact some of the businesses near you to offer your services.

MAIL FORWARDING SERVICE

Although the post office does offer a mail forwarding service, it is often slow and not satisfactory for someone who is away for only a few weeks' vacation.

Most people don't want to impose on friends to perform this service but are not satisfied with the post office service. These people are ready customers for a mail forwarding business and are happy to pay a fee for the service.

There are people, also, who prefer, for one reason or another, not to make their home address known and want to keep one specific mailing address while they travel to other areas. They use a mail forwarding service all year round. In either case you can charge a fee of from $10 to $50 a month depending on the amount of mail to be forwarded.

Some businessmen must operate from several different

addresses without having an office secretary in each location. They, too, are customers for a mail forwarding service. Here your fee could be from $25 to $100 a month.

Advertise your service in newspapers and trade magazines and through direct contact. You should be able to develop a good clientele if your ads are placed where they reach enough people. Metropolitan areas are best suited to this type of business.

STENOGRAPHIC SERVICES

All metropolitan cities support several public stenographers, a number of which operate out of well-located business offices. Many of these businesses, however, started in an unpretentious manner.

This function is ideally suited to the stenographer who wants to begin his or her operation at home. I did this myself several years ago without any equipment other than a used typewriter, stand and chair, costing $115.

I started with one customer who furnished the Dictaphone equipment. He brought his recordings to my house every morning for transcription and picked up the completed copy every night.

If there is one satisfied customer who can bring more to your door, it's easy to build a sizeable business from nothing. I made $2 an hour, but it is possible to make $3.50 to $4 an hour today. You can find customers for this service among small businesses, salesmen and other single operators who don't work from an office.

By individual contact, classified ads and word-of-mouth advertising you can build a good paying business in your home which can easily expand to a full-time profitable office operation.

HOW TO PUT YOUR TELEPHONE TO WORK FOR YOU

With a bit of ingenuity you can discover a wide range of opportunities for making money from your telephone.

There are many sales organizations that pay people to call prospective customers and set up appointments for them. Many of these prefer to have this done in their offices, but you can promote doing it in your home for many businesses that have never used such a service before.

HOUSEWIFE PROVIDES SERVICE TO CAR DEALERS

Some car dealers provide a special service to their new car customers—calling every month or so to see if all is well with the new car. Jean R., a housewife, offered this service to car dealers and other businesses selling merchandise that requires regular upkeep at the rate of 75¢ a call. This brought in from $7 to $9 an hour.

OTHER NEEDED SERVICES

Families having a sick or elderly member who has to be left alone during the day will gladly pay someone a small fee for regular calls during the day. The calls provide a "friendly visit" type of contact to alleviate loneliness and also serve as a check to see that everything is all right. A classified ad will bring customers for this service.

There are a number of small businesses that need an answering service a few hours during the day, and yet can't afford the going rate. You could take on a few of these accounts and earn a small supplementary income from them. Lucille K. did this and earned $110 a month for extra spending money. The secret here is finding and filling a need.

YOUR EVERYDAY EQUIPMENT CAN EARN YOU MONEY

Most of these services can be operated with equipment you already have in your home: there is little need to purchase anything.

Many have typewriters. For those who don't, there are quite a few opportunities to do by hand what someone else would do on a typewriter.

Your telephone, a table, chair and shelves or fruit crates can handle many of the businesses suggested here. An inexpensive manually operated typewriter is an added advantage.

LETTER WRITING—BUSINESS AND PERSONAL

The ability to write a good letter is almost as specialized a skill as any writing done for the general public. Someone who can write good letters for others should have no trouble finding clients.

I have done a great deal of this myself and earned from $100 to $125 in a week. For some time, I answered letters for a man who was constantly called upon for personal advice. I grew to know him well and to understand his philosophy so completely that he had difficulty distinguishing between the letters he wrote and those I wrote for him. He did, in fact, frequently ask me, "Did I write this or did you?"

The secret here is developing an ability to express yourself in someone else's style, and offering your services to many busy people who seldom find time to answer their mail. There are many who never answer letters—especially personal ones—but who would like to keep in communication with relatives and friends.

HOW TO FIND YOUR CUSTOMERS

Advertise your personalized letter service through classified ads and by direct contact with people you know in clubs, churches and other organizations.

There is a need, also, for a similar service in many small one-man business operations. The business proprietor needs more than a mere typist. He needs someone who can word the letter properly as well.

The field is wide open. If you have the skill, determination and persistence, you will have customers waiting at your door. Talk to people, write to small businesses and advertise in local publications. It's an untapped field—develop it.

BOOKKEEPING WITH SOMETHING ADDED

G. E. Schaff, a retired navy commander, took a job teaching in a business college and studied accounting and tax law on the side. Later he took a job with a tax consultant firm. When the owner of the tax firm retired, Schaff started a business of his own in his home. Many of the tax firm's clients sought him out.

In his own business he is much more than just a bookkeeper or a tax man. He is also a financial affairs troubleshooter for his clients—far beyond the usual responsibilities of a bookkeeper. He specializes in accounts of older people. Many of his clients are widows who depend on him completely for the handling of their financial affairs. His business is not exclusively for older people with limited savings and incomes, for he does a great deal of business with contractors and other big business operations. One of the secrets to his success is giving special attention to people who are not experienced enough in the field of tax laws and general finance to protect their own interests adequately.

His home office setup is ideally suited to this type of business: many clients like to stay and chat awhile in his office which is just off a big living room in his home. They can sit in either place to rest or visit. Most of his clients have consulted him from eight to fifteen years, and are now much more than business acquaintances. They are his personal friends.

OFFERING INDIVIDUALIZED SERVICE

An example of Schaff's individualized handling of a client's affairs is the service he gave a man who was referred to him after acquiring a piece of property. Since that time Schaff has directed this man through several transactions involving the original purchase, enabling his client to realize considerable equity gains and a secure financial future.

This could be a very profitable business for any capable and conscientious accountant or bookkeeper, Schaff says. If you are knowledgeable in accounting and tax laws, have other people's interests at heart and are willing to work for those interests, this could be the business for you.

Schaff is not greedy for money and doesn't charge the top fee, but he says it would be easy for someone charging the current rates to earn as much as $15,000 a year working part-time. That would mean working full time during the tax season and very short hours the rest of the year. The income would increase considerably, perhaps doubling, if you want to operate it on a full-time year-round basis.

Vitally important to this business is the ability to demonstrate your reliability as well as your capability to this type of clientele. Many such people have been "taken" too many times, and are suspicious of anyone wanting to handle their financial affairs. The secret to a very lucrative and satisfying business in this area is establishing your reputation and being willing to give extra service.

HOW TO FIND UNUSUAL OPPORTUNITIES FOR TYPISTS

A home typing service can be a highly profitable business if handled correctly. You must solicit the right kind of work. There isn't enough money in doing a single letter or document for a variety of customers. Volume jobs are the answer.

Student term papers and some letter jobs provide good sources of income and fulfill the volume criteria. Lucy P. set up her own typing business in between temporary secretarial jobs. She did a good business with student papers, but she had some unusual customers for letters as well. One customer had her type one letter 90 times addressing it to a different person each time.

If you are in a location where it is possible to put up a shingle and present a professional appearance, it is easy to charge at least $6 an hour. But if your business must be done more unobtrusively in your own home, the charge is usually by the page, ranging from 45¢ to 75¢ a page.

DEVELOPING YOUR ACCOUNTS

Volume business is still available from lawyers, certified public accountants, insurance and construction companies.

Canvass lawyers' buildings for legal papers from attorneys: there is a lot of untapped business for typists in legal offices. Most of these papers are several pages long. Certified public accountants offer good territory for typists, especially around tax time. Insurance companies frequently need extra typists for policies. Construction company bid typing is another area worth exploring. The secret to building this kind of business is going from office to office in buildings that house these professional people. You will be able to develop a steady clientele in a short period of time among these professions.

OFFERING SPECIAL SERVICES TO WRITERS

There have been many times over the years when I was working on a book manuscript or other writing project—after my regular working hours—when I found it extremely difficult to do all the necessary research. I tried having someone else do this work for me, but never really found a good research person. If you have a knack for this type of work, you will find many eager customers among freelance writers, especially those who do their writing while working other jobs.

This could lead you into various areas of research. In addition to book research you might be called upon to conduct interviews for special information needed by an author. The ability to ask the right questions and to know when you have the correct answers is important here. This field can be exciting as well as profitable.

There are many writers who send out a number of manuscripts every week requiring a great deal of record-keeping. The writer needs to know where and when he or she sent each manuscript and when the manuscripts were accepted or rejected. Not too many writers enjoy routine recording; it might be a profitable occupation for you if you do like it. You would need to find writers not too far from your home, and this might limit prospects. But if you do know where to locate writers near you and are a detail organizer, it's an excellent opportunity.

PROVIDING A UNIQUE SERVICE FOR JOB APPLICANTS

A temporary employment service in a metropolitan city offers a rather unique job opportunity to residents of the smaller communities on the outskirts of the city itself. Employment services sometimes hire interviewers in these communities to interview job applicants in their homes. Agencies have discovered that many potential temporary employees are great for the work available to them, but won't travel great distances to find the jobs. These are the people they reach through neighborhood interviewers.

If you live in a community near a larger metropolitan area, you may want to contact temporary employment agencies in the city to offer your services as a neighborhood interviewer. Laura B., a housewife, did this and earned $300 a month part-time.

If this is a whole new concept to some of these agencies, it might be a good opportunity to pioneer such a program in your community.

If you find it is new to some of the agencies you contact, you may want to offer your services to them in finding neighborhood interviewers in other communities. You can charge either the agency or the applicants who are hired as interviewers 20 percent to 30 percent of the first month's salary.

SECRETS OF DISCOVERING THE GREATEST NEEDS

The greatest need for part-time clerical and secretarial help is among small business operations having less than three employees. Survey some of the larger successful businesses in your community to uncover services they are using which have been effective and profitable. Talk to managers and owners, asking their assistance in finding the information you need. People like to be asked for information. It is the highest form of compliment you can pay them, so don't be bashful. Tell them your needs and why you are asking for their help.

Once you have a good list of the types of services a business needs, decide which you are best qualified to offer. If there are several you can handle, so much the better.

Now you will need to find a market for your services. To do this check with the Small Business Administration for names and addresses of all the small businesses in your area. SBA business consultants will also be able to direct you to other sources of information regarding small business operations in your community.

Once you have the list and have decided on the various services you are prepared to give, write a convincing sales letter offering your services. Have an offset print shop run off as many copies as you need for your list.

After the firms have had adequate time to receive your letter, a personal call or visit from you would be in order. If your letter presented your case well and your services were offered at a price that a small business finds equitable, you will uncover a number of new customers. Word-of-mouth advertising beyond that point will help you expand.

HOW TO FIND THE RIGHT CUSTOMERS—ALL YOU NEED

When Martha. P., a secretary, retired, she developed a business from experiences and acquaintances she had acquired in her years of clerical work.

Her own experience had taught her that busy executives don't have time to remember such important dates as renewal time for passports, insurance policies and driver's licenses. She set up a special reminder service and got her first 100 customers by making a telephone call to every executive she recalled from her days as a secretary. She then gave simple brochures to everyone she had called and asked if they would tell others about her service.

In a short period of time Martha had increased her business sevenfold with practically no investment other than her efforts.

The secret of her success in finding all the customers she could handle was that she utilized her numerous contacts from over the years as a secretary.

HOW TO DEVELOP YOUR OWN CONTACTS

If you or any members of your family have worked in some position where you came in contact with a lot of business people, you have a ready-made list of prospective customers for your special service to small businesses.

If you don't have many contacts you still can take advantage of the best kind of advertising in the world—word-of-mouth. Anything you can do to get people to tell others of what you have to offer is a sure way to acquire customers. It is sometimes wise to devise the situation which will start this word-of-mouth advertising for your service. You can do this easily by selecting a few individuals in your community who know a lot of people and who have the respect of those they know. Give these community leaders a sample of your service. Do it for them without cost and ask them to tell others about it. If necessary, you can pay them a small percentage to do this for you; but if your service is superior and much desired, you won't need to pay anyone to tell others about it.

I have had excellent success with another method when I wanted to promote something. I mentioned it to everyone I thought might have even the slightest interest, usually asking them for help in getting the word about. When you have something worth offering, you will find that most people are eager to help you promote it. This can be done very successfully, but it does need to be handled with finesse—very casually. If it ever becomes a nuisance thing to people, you are lost. Mention your product or service only in casual discussions and where, if at all possible, it fits into the general conversation of the moment.

You can be sure of all the customers you want by using any one of these approaches that fits your particular situation or, better yet, if you use ALL of them at one time or another.

THREE RULES THAT GUARANTEE REPEAT CUSTOMERS

Once you have succeeded in acquiring your first customers you can be sure of their continued business if you follow three simple rules:

1. Give the finest service available, accurately and promptly.
2. Give it with a spirit of friendliness no matter what the situation.
3. Give each customer individual attention as if he or she were the most important one on your books.

RECEPTIONIST BECOMES PRODUCER OF LOCAL TV SHOW

Clerical work is often the door that leads to a top executive position. It is open to the worker who has foresight and ability to prepare and plan for the opportunity on the other side.

Diane Kalas was a secretary, a housewife, a receptionist and finally the producer of her own television show.

Watching TV at home one day she saw someone do a television interview and decided that it was something she could do. This was an ambition she had had since her early school days. Immediately she visualized herself in such a role and set it as a target. She then took the steps necessary to reach it. She enrolled in a radio and television class at a local college and, as part of the course, worked in the college radio station doing interviews.

After many attempts to get a job at the television station that carried the interview show she was hired as a receptionist and news reporter. She told them she would do anything, even scrub floors, if she could have a chance "on camera" along with whatever job they gave her. Within one short month she was co-hosting the show and three months later, when the producer of "Today in Arizona" was promoted, she was placed in his position. The secret to her success was strong determination and a willingness to do whatever was needed to get the job.

HOW TO FIND YOUR OWN NICHE

If you have clerical skills but would like to move into other professions, take a look around you and decide what you want. You, too, can do what Diane did. Solicit clerical work in the firms or organizations that offer the greatest opportunity in the profession you'd like to try. Once you are on the inside, take every opportunity to prove your ability and make good use of those opportunities.

5

*Turning Your Hobbies
into a Profitable
Second Income*

The Thorndike Barnhart dictionary defines a hobby as "something a person especially likes to work at or study which is not his main business or occupation; favorite pastime."

What more ideal situation is there than earning a livelihood working at your favorite pastime, doing something you especially enjoy? Second-income occupations starting from an enjoyable hobby often develop into such profitable operations that they become a person's full-time business activity. Frequently this allows an individual to leave a humdrum, uninteresting job to spend all his time doing what he wants to do.

The secret of finding such an opportunity is to work at hobbies you enjoy, perfecting your skill as much as you can. We spend at least one-third of our waking hours and at least half of our lifetime earning a living. Why not spend that time doing what we like? Turning an enjoyable hobby into a productive business operation is one of the best ways I know for doing this. It can be the direct road to earning big money with little effort. When you are doing what you enjoy your efforts no longer seem like work.

MATCHING YOUR HOBBIES TO NEEDS IN YOUR COMMUNITY

The secret of making your hobby profitable is to recognize that in this busy world there are many people who would rather pay someone else to do certain chores than take the time and effort to do them themselves. This is true even in leisure activities. Some needs of others might easily fit your particular hobby interests. The secret is to keep your eyes open and to talk with friends, acquaintances and almost anyone you happen to meet to discover many of these needs.

I don't like to give much time to detail work and am happy to pay someone else to handle record-keeping and other details for me. Some people find it difficult to select gifts for relatives or friends and would welcome help in this throughout the year.

MAKING GOOD MONEY FROM SAMPLE DISPLAYS

There are retail shops that pay individuals to make display boards for various types of merchandise. This is particularly true with hobby merchandise. There are all kinds of kits for sale in hobby shops, and customers like to see the finished product.

One way of making extra money might be to make samples from kits. If you are particularly adept at working with some of the materials in these kits or just good at working with your hands generally, check the hobby stores in your community. You should find a number of kits that fit your hobbies.

You can develop a profitable business in your home making these sample displays. There is no cost involved for you, as the stores furnish all the material and pay you a specific amount for each sample. It is possible, depending on the amount of time you put into it, to make as much as $10,000 a year doing this in your home.

PACKAGING FOR HOBBY SHOPS

Hobby shops also pay individuals to do packaging of hobby materials in their home—stamp packets, bags of beads, marbles, etc.—paying a specific amount for each piece. You can make, according to your speed, $2 or more an hour at this. Again, no investment is required.

HOW TO TURN LEISURE FUN ACTIVITIES INTO CASH

You probably have indulged in a variety of hobbies over the years for fun and relaxation. People do this all through their lives, never thinking of receiving financial rewards for any of it. Since most of us, in this day of rising costs, could use some extra income, it might be well to take a look at your hobby activity. It could provide that extra cash you need.

Taking on another job is out of the question in many cases

because of the additional time involved. But there's a secret source of time—you are already spending it on your hobby activity. The only additional time required is what it takes to market the product or the service.

There are a lot of men—young and old—who like to *make* airplanes or railway layouts. Assembling the materials is their hobby. At the same time, there are other men who want to *fly* these planes or *operate* a railway layout but don't want to bother to make the product. The two groups need to get together. The best way to do this is through a hobby shop.

MODEL AIRPLANES BRING GOOD MONEY FOR HOBBYIST

Bert G. made model airplanes—non-motored and motored. The non-motored planes cost him from $2 to $18 and the motored ones, $12 to $70. He sold these in finished form for double the cost to him.

If your hobby is making any of these rather intricate products, check with the hobby shops near you. They will be able to supply you with customers. This means you can make a lot of airplanes, railway layouts or whatever. Not only will your hobby cost you nothing, but it will earn you money as well.

EARNING A MAJOR PROFIT FROM A MINOR SKILL

Dee Gordon, with his wife, put together a simple chain of safety pins, then developed a variety of designs for necklaces. He offered these to a manufacturing firm which bought the idea for hobby kits and agreed to pay royalties to the Gordons. When approximately $300,000 worth of kits were sold in one year, Gordon realized a good percentage in royalties—an excellent return for no effort and virtually no investment. That was only a beginning. His profits have continued to grow as these jewelry kits, known as "Pin-Tastics," have increased in popularity, He now has bought out the manufacturer.

Gordon advises others who have a good kit idea to look into his method of marketing. It is the safest and easiest way to make a profit from your hobby idea and free your time to take on another equally profitable project.

Many hobbyists miss this point completely, Gordon says. They think they should not give anything to anyone—a manufacturer, wholesaler or any sales outlet—and should do it all themselves, keeping all the profits. Most amateurs, however, don't have enough real knowledge of what it costs to put a kit together and then promote it. Going through an established manufacturing firm eliminates all the problems of setting up your own business and provides a sizeable profit because of the larger volume of sales. It takes none of the hobbyist's time or effort. The manufacturing firm does it all.

If you have a good idea, check it out with your nearby hobby shop for possible sale to a manufacturer. You will find this the most profitable way to go.

HOW TO ASSURE YOUR SUCCESS

Before you turn your hobby into a business operation, learn all you can about that kind of business. Discover everything possible about manufacturing, markups and what it costs to "kit" an item. This latter includes such things as artwork on the box, "shrink wrap" and the box itself.

It is essential that you know how to price your merchandise so you won't come out on the losing end. Make sure your markup is adequate—at least double your cost—or you will soon be out of business. The secret of succeeding is to develop the ability to recognize all the costs, some of which are hidden.

Again, I suggest you talk with the owners of hobby shops in your vicinity. Most people are more than happy to help someone else get a start even when the person is going into a similar or competitive business. In your case you are going to supply items to be sold. Your business could easily make you a steady hobby shop customer. Talk with them and learn all you can from their experiences.

The Small Business Administration offers free consultation services to small business operations. Talk to their consultants, too, and get any information they have available on the subject.

Your venture doesn't have to be a gamble if you follow these simple rules: Produce a good and desired product or service, and make yourself thoroughly knowledgeable of the business before you start. There are many highly successful business people who started with small hobby operations. You can do it too.

FROM PART-TIME HOBBY TO SUCCESSFUL BUSINESS OPERATION

Carl P. turned a small plot of land—a little over an acre in size—into a profitable business operation. His hobby was raising bees. He developed, from this hobby, two interesting sidelines, both highly profitable.

From material developed by the bees to feed their queens, he manufactures royal jelly—a product to which he attributes almost magical health benefits. He wholesales this to vitamin manufacturers, cosmetic companies and doctors who, in turn, sell it for a better than 100 percent markup. This sideline alone has become big business for its originator.

Carl earns an additional income by renting his bees to fruit crop growers where bee pollination is necessary before the crops can mature.

He not only can make as much as $30,000 a year from these two projects but he keeps all the honey himself, and his business operating expenses are almost nil. It costs nothing to feed the bees, and there is no upkeep involved.

You can secure detailed information on beekeeping business opportunities by writing to the Superintendent of Documents, U.S. Government Printing Office, Washington, D.C. 20402. Ask for their publications on honey bees.

MAKING YOUR OWN GIFTS FOR SALE

There are a number of people who make their own birthday, anniversary, Christmas and other special occasion gifts. You can turn this craft into a profitable operation. It is an ideal start for a money-making business in your home.

If you are interested in making some extra money for yourself by making gifts, take a look at your immediate advantages. You already have tested products to offer, because you know how people react to the items you make. You may be good at creating children's furniture, doll houses, cabinets or interesting knick-knacks that delight your friends and family. Whatever you've been making for gifts, if you've had enthusiastic responses from those on the receiving end, you can be sure you have a salable product.

My sister made a rather unique poncho for all the female members of her family when ponchos were at the height of their popularity, and we were all eager to receive such a choice gift. She could have made a good second income from that item alone if she had placed it on the market. It cost her less than $5 to make; comparable ponchos in the stores were selling for $15 or more.

PIPE HOBBY BECOMES PROFITABLE ENTERPRISE

Allen F. made pipes for himself and as gifts for friends and family as a hobby. When someone would see a friend smoking one of these pipes, invariably they'd ask where it was purchased. Before he knew it Allen found himself in the pipe-making business for profit. His cost was minimal since he had no special equipment and he picked up the wood from the land around him. He sold some of his pipes for as much as $50.

TEN GOOD-SELLING GIFT ITEMS

There is an endless list of gift items that cost just a few dollars to make yet bring a 100 percent or more profit, all of which are easy to market. The following are a few from the list:

1. Lamps made from popsickle sticks. The ones I've seen look like something made in the orient. They can be put together in exotic shapes to fit a variety of home interiors.

2. Magnet foam figures. All kinds of objects—flowers, owls, fish, animals—what have you—are cut from foam rubber material. A magnet is placed on the back so they will stick to metal—refrigerators, stoves, cabinets and other metal appliances.

3. Macramé items. This art dates back to the Phoenicians but has been revived in recent years. Quick-selling items are wall hangers, belts, necklaces, pot slings and even room dividers.

4. Decoupage. There are many varieties of gift items made from this craft in three-dimensional, single dimension and dome techniques. Decoupaged old books make unusual and decorative pieces, and decoupaged wedding invitations sell well. This is an especially good field for custom-made gift items.

5. Dip-and-drape figures. These are made of cloth saturated in a material similar to pre-starch. The finished product is usually a figurine.

6. Fake fur flowers. Flowers are made in a variety of shapes and sizes from fur-like material and often held in place by a bit of hair spray.

7. Bottles. All shapes and sizes can be trimmed with anything you may have around the house. They can be made into lamps, vases and other popular gift items to enhance their salability.

8. Chenille flowers. These are made of bump chenille—just like the material used for pipe cleaners only with a bump in it.

9. Candle craft. Every scent you can think of, every color and all shapes and sizes are on the market today. This can be a highly profitable business if you use enough ingenuity in your designs.

10. String art. This has been revived from a very ancient art. Sail boat models with the sails made of string are very beautiful. Your imagination can create a variety of geometrical designs for wall hangings and other decorative pieces.

Instructions for these crafts and materials are available at most hobby shops where you can also get suggestions as to the best ways to sell these products at a profit.

OPERATING A SHOPPING SERVICE

Shopping is a recreational activity for many people, but other people have no time or interest in it. For those who enjoy it there is a golden opportunity to earn some good second-income money.

I have friends who go every week to a special shop-and-swap marketplace. They do it for the fun of it whether they need to buy anything or not. Frequently they purchase needed items for friends or relatives.

If this is a spare time hobby of yours, why not turn it into profit by offering to do other people's shopping at the same time for a fee? Look for customers among busy working people, highly involved society people, residents of adult apartment complexes and senior citizens.

PROVIDING SERVICE TO SHUT-INS

If one of your hobbies is doing little things for people less fortunate than you, why not turn it into profit by expanding your services to a regular part-time vocation?

Not everyone can afford the time to do this sort of thing on a daily basis without remuneration, and there is nothing wrong with earning your living serving others. If there was, we wouldn't have nurses, doctors or any professionals who are paid to do things for others.

When my mother was confined to her home, with no outside activities allowed, and I was working every day, I was happy to pay someone $3 or $4 to visit her for even half an hour each day. I'm sure you can find all the customers you can handle if you advertise this service in your local papers. With four to six other confined people in close proximity to each other you can easily make from $12 to $16 daily working two to three hours.

Many people can't afford to pay someone to stay with a member of their family all the time, but the burden could be relieved considerably by short daily visits such as this. Finding clients who live fairly close to each other eliminates unprofitable traveling time.

TURNING YOUR CAR INTO A GOOD MONEY-EARNER

It was equally important to me, when my mother was ill, to find someone who could take her to the doctor sometimes two or three days a week. I paid individuals $2.50 an hour to do this when I could find a person available, but much of the time I had to take a few hours away from work to handle the situation.

This is a much-needed service which should bring a number of customers if properly promoted.

An added function which is needed almost as much as the taxi service to doctors is one offering pleasure rides for people who live alone and never get a change of scenery.

There are many ways you can use your car for special services and turn a people-helping hobby into a remunerative and rewarding business operation.

SPECIAL PROJECTS WITH WOOD

Hobby shops frequently have customers seeking special wood products such as custom-made inlaid chess boards to fit a specific size. Others need special boards on which to mount medals or special trophies.

This type of work requires a fully equipped woodworking shop that would take from $300 to $500 to set up. If you have this particular talent or are already engaged in woodworking as a hobby, check hobby shops for special customers such as these. You may find a whole new specialized market for your woodworking hobby.

A business in wood which has had special appeal to professional photographers and artists was started by Raidy Stetson in Phoenix, Arizona. It's the Frame-It-Yourself Shop. The customers of this shop frame their own pictures and buy only materials from the shop. Everything is provided for making the frames, including tools and expert assistance, and the customer gets the frame at half the normal cost. This unique idea has taken hold so well that Stetson is considering the possibility of opening a second store. It cost him $20,000 to start, half of which came from a bank loan. The business will bring as much as $30,000 gross income annually. The secret of the appeal of this business is its do-it-yourself customer-saving aspect.

MAKING ARTWORK PAY BIG PROFITS

There are a great many opportunities for talented commercial artists to make top money if they have the ability to sell themselves and their work. Many business managers don't realize their need for a commercial artist until it is brought to their attention. If an artist is able to see a need and can demonstrate visually his or her ability to fill that need, there are many good customers waiting for those services.

Fine art is an entirely different area, but it, too, can be highly profitable, especially for the artist who has something unusual to offer.

WELDER-ARTIST

George J. creates some beautiful pieces of art without paint or paint brushes, and sells his work for as much as $300. He welds nails, railroad spikes, welding rods, nuts, bolts and all kinds of scrap metal into landscapes, geometric figures and figurines. His work is sold in exclusive gift shops and gift departments and in top calibre art galleries. He has also had one-man shows in some of the galleries.

The material he uses cost very little because so much of it is scrap metal and the equipment for such work can be purchased for as little as $20. More elaborate welding equipment can be purchased later if necessary, but a small inexpensive set does quite well for this type of work.

PROVIDING SPECIAL INTERIOR DECORATING SERVICES

Interior decorating is a special art in itself which requires not only a natural gift for artistic color and arrangement combinations but also a great deal of specialized training and knowledge.

To become a fully qualified professional interior decorator you need to take a four-year course and then work for four more years under a qualified interior decorator.

The schooling can be handled on a part-time basis through one of the recognized correspondence schools such as the Chicago School of Interior Design or LaSalle Extension University. Once you have qualified yourself, opportunities for a highly profitable business which can be operated from your home are excellent. It is possible to develop a business in this field which will bring you anywhere from $25,000 to $100,000 a year.

OTHER ALLIED FIELDS

If it isn't your ambition to become a fully qualified interior decorator, there are still special interior decorating services that can be provided by someone with artistic abilities.

Some artists have developed a special talent for adapting their paintings to specific home interiors and make good incomes doing specially commissioned paintings to fit specific surroundings. If you have a special gift for flower arrangements this is another art that can be developed into a highly professional skill.

There are many areas for the artist to perform a service which compliments the work of a professional interior decorator. The best way to develop this business is through word-of-mouth advertising. If you can do it for a friend, he or she will tell others, and your business will grow in accordance with the quality of the service rendered.

OFFERING SOMETHING DIFFERENT IN PUBLIC RELATIONS

Public relations can be the combination of several different hobbies. It entails ability in journalistic writing, photography, artwork, promotion and the art of working with professional and nonprofessional people. A well-qualified professional can freelance, charging from $10 to $20 an hour.

Public relations work usually requires specialized training, but a person who has been involved in some of these hobbies has the potential for developing the skill.

If you do have the background and want to become a better-than-average freelance public relations specialist, the secret is to offer an innovative approach to prospective customers.

In one of my public relations positions I worked for a non-profit antipoverty agency which was geared largely to helping the less advantaged learn to help themselves. There was a great deal of community interest in the program, and I decided to organize a special public relations advisory committee made up of newspaper, radio, television and public relations professionals. After starting with a small group—eight people—representing the areas mentioned, we later more than doubled that number. These people became much more than an advisory group. They were an all-out action group. Together we developed some huge city-wide promotions and one of the finest public relations programs in the city. The secret here was combining my resources with those of many other professionals in the area.

A committee such as this is not feasible if you are working with strictly commercial accounts, but it is ideal for a non-profit community program. There are many community-minded industries and businesses, some of which have community improvement programs as part of their operations. These types of programs and most non-profit organizations would lend themselves to this kind of a public relations committee. It can greatly enhance your accomplishments either in a regular public relations job or as a freelancer.

SOMETHING DIFFERENT IN GIFT WRAPPING

Most larger stores have giftwrapping services, but there are many small stores which do not. These stores—especially those that do a sizeable business in gift merchandise—could use a special giftwrapping service. It wouldn't be practical for an individual to move from one store to another wrapping gifts at these places, but you might sell them boxes that are already gift wrapped. You can set up an assortment of various size boxes, cover the lids and the bottoms separtely with attractive gift wrapping paper and place bows or other decoration on the lids. The shops charge for these boxes just as they do for special gift wrapping in the larger stores. All the store personnel have to add to the packaged gift is two small pieces of scotch tape if they want the box held tightly shut.

The store owners and managers won't be out any money in offering this service to customers, and they'd make a lot of people happy. I have purchased gifts many times in stores where there is no gift wrapping, and it's a great inconvenience for me because I don't like to wrap things. A service like this offers a wide open market for some enterprising, artistic man or woman. If this describes you, why not do it?

MAKING PERSONALIZED GREETING CARDS

Personalized Christmas cards have been popular for a long time. Why not extend this to year-round greeting cards?

Photographs of individuals, babies or families have been used a great deal at Christmas time. Gay. G. put together samples of this personalized type of card in a box assortment for birthdays, special holidays, anniversaries, get well and other occasions. She included in the assortment a special order blank for Christmas cards with a photograph furnished by the customer. Gay took orders by showing her sample card assortment. The cost for this varies according to the type of paper used and the price you pay for printing. Shop around for the best buy in both areas and charge the customer double your cost.

This can be done using portraits by an artist, a family coat of arms or a special lettering design for name or initials as well. The important thing is that the design and handling be distinctive, attractive and out of the ordinary. Gay placed sample boxes in card shops, gift stores and department stores. The stores received 33 1/3 percent on all orders. This same idea is also very effective for businesses as an advertising medium.

TOUR GUIDING WITH AN UNUSUAL TWIST

When tourists come to any city they usually see more than the natives see in twenty or thirty years. Sponsoring tours of sites in your own state or city for local clubs, schools and individuals is a flourishing business if properly promoted. This might be advertised as a "See Your Own Home Town" or "Know Your State" tour. Promote the idea, for a fee, to all the organizations in your city or state—young people's groups, senior citizens, political groups, school children—the market is unlimited.

"RECYCLING" THROWN AWAY ITEMS FOR SALE

There are several good books on this subject that tell you what you can do with almost anything you normally throw away. You should be able to find some of these books in your local library.

You can make useful, salable items from toilet paper rolls, bleach jugs, beer and pop cans—anything. "Trim your trash" is the motto of many hobbyists today.

Tin cans make all kinds of art items. Dan W. makes World War I airplanes from tin cans. I read in our local paper about a man who is building houses from tin cans. He uses cans in a six pack and makes blocks from them. They make a very sturdy, substantial building, according to the report. The basic unit is said to withstand a 4,000 pound weight.

Burl C. started visiting junkyards to pick up things he could repair for his own use or sell. His business soon grew to such an extent he gave up a good salaried job and now makes a minimum of $150 a day in this recycling business.

OPERATING CRAFTS SALES SHOP FOR NEIGHBORHOOD

Before you set up an actual retail crafts shop in your home you should check the zoning laws for that area as well as local merchandising regulations. If you are not located where you can set up such a shop to sell your neighbors' crafts, you can merchandise them in much the same way that Avon cosmetics are handled. Take some samples around to the neighbors and tell them about other items, then take orders to be delivered later.

An excellent way to handle a crafts shop that will not only profit you and your neighboring craftsmen but will help the overall community as well is establishment of a charity-promotion shop. You and your suppliers would agree, on this basis, to turn over half your profits to some charitable program. You would need to find out which programs need funds and which you feel are the most deserving, and then promote all your sales along these lines. You will do a flourishing business and have the satisfaction of knowing you are helping others do as well.

OFFERING A SPECIAL SIGN SERVICE

Many small store operations post price signs that are crude, amateurish and unattractive.

Hobby store owner Dee Gordon had this problem in his own store and decided to get a variety of price signs printed. He was so pleased with the results that he decided to box and sell them. A box of 100 assorted price signs which sold for $10 turned out to be a good sales item.

Talk to people in various small business operations and look around the shops. Discover their needs and produce the product.

OPPORTUNITIES EVERYWHERE

The opportunities for you to earn good money from your hobby are unlimited. I have given you only a few examples in this chapter, but they are all around you. Opportunity isn't around the corner—it's right in front of you. Take the ball and run with it.

6

Innovative Ways to
Food-Making Profits

Food preparation is a creative art; the work of a culinary artist can be as exciting and rewarding as creating works with paint and brush. There is a wide open market in this field for both the novice and the expert, and opportunities to develop productive second-income businesses from the kitchen are available to men and women alike. It is a profession in which many a beginner has become a master, for it offers a ready opportunity for small, easily acquired jobs that grow bigger according to a person's ability and determination.

Robert Bland, executive chef for the Arizona Biltmore Hotel, started this way. He began at age 15 doing pantry work during his school vacation. His first summer he worked only at serving desserts, but the second and third years he made buffet salads and dressings and worked as assistant to the top man.

In college, while studying to become a certified public accountant, he continued to work in pantries each summer, this time doing resort work in the Grand Tetons of Wyoming. He started as head pantry man, and then did relief for pantry personnel—an excellent way to become knowledgeable in all areas. By this time he had discovered a highly profitable profession in the culinary arts, so he set aside his CPA plans and went into cooking as a full-time profession. Today he is the executive chef for one of the best known resort hotels in the southwest.

UNREVEALED METHODS FOR MAKING DAILY ACTIVITY PAY

Bev Barney turned her daily activites into a thriving and exciting business out of her home. She began watching television from time to time when she was forced to stay home and off her feet for a long time after a serious operation. One day she happened to watch a program where prizes were given for recipes.

Bev didn't think the recipes were that good, so she sent in 26 recipes of her own, underlining the ingredients the TV program was promoting. She won six weeks in a row, getting all kinds of prizes—hams, cases of salad dressing, etc., as well as money.

Other viewers began to complain when Bev kept winning, so the program director, Bee Beyer of "Cooking Around the World," offered her a job writing for the show. Bev started writing regularly for the program, taking her own recipes and putting specific products into them—those advertised on the program. "I'm not a good writer," Bev says, "but I am a good cook."

Bev made many suggestions for product promotion such as advising people to use milk instead of water in their cake mixes, thereby selling more milk, and at the same time helping cake mix customers make better cakes.

While she was writing for the TV show she also took on a job as food editor for three weeklies in the area. Here she started consulting well-known personalities, seeking out their favorite recipes or foods.

Bev worked with Bee Beyer for 18 months, learning a great deal during that time. She then had to give up the job to move to Arizona for family health reasons. Here, she and her husband invested a small inheritance in a business venture and lost about $90,000. Since it was necessary to start all over again, Bev turned to her food background and began to recoup the losses. She started a food column in several local weeklies, appeared several times on local TV programs and submitted numerous recipes to the programs. She started doing volunteer public relations work for a women's professional club which led to a paid promotional job with the local March of Dimes program. Here she used her food ideas to raise funds, and began developing food recipes to help promote local food company products.

Bev Barney started, in those early days of her career, making every activity in her day pay dividends, and she has never stopped.

When she reads a magazine, walks down the street and sees a food firm, or goes shopping and sees a new product, she takes full advantage of it. For example, in the market when she sees such a product, she calls or writes the distributor. In doing this she uses the professional title of food stylist and professional letterheads and business cards which enhance her credentials. She tells the firm she is freelancing and asks if she can experiment with their product in her test kitchen and come up with a new recipe. The firm agrees to pay her for any recipe used to promote their product. Her test kitchen is the same kitchen in which she does her everyday cooking.

Bev does recipes for a local frozen food manufacturer, writes for several papers, does an annual cookbook for one of the papers, puts out flyers and brochures and secures newspaper advertising for products included in her recipes. She also publicizes recipes of many well-known personalities who frequently give her information for a personality article that sells to a national magazine. Sometimes she researches the history of a particular food and sells an article based on her findings.

Bev has built her home business into a $1,000 or more monthly income and, even in the beginning, never made less than $500. This business requires little investment in money. It is based almost entirely on her ability to capitalize on daily activities.

HIDDEN WAYS TO TURN FREE MOMENTS INTO PROFIT

Low-carbohydrate diets have become increasingly popular in recent years, yet food manufacturers and restaurants have been slow in catching up with the trend. Special diet meals at most restaurants cater only to the low-calorie advocate. The same is true of frozen and canned foods.

Enterprising culinary experts saw the potential market in low-calorie preparations several years ago and developed highly profitable businesses in this field. The more recent leaning toward low-carbohydrate diets offers the same challenge and opportunity with a whole new group of eager customers.

I know several private cooks who are having a lot of fun exploring new ways to make old dishes with a low carbohydrate count combined with pleasant taste. For those of you who are experimenting with some of these new recipes in your home there's a golden opportunity to turn that activity into cash. With very little added effort you could prepare these special diet dishes for restaurants or for grocery stores in frozen form. If you don't want to cook in the quantities necessary for sale, why not experiment in your kitchen and develop recipes for these special diets to sell in book form or to special restaurants, magazines or newspapers? It's a brand new field, hardly tapped at all. Why don't you pioneer it?

CAKE DECORATING EXPANDED TO BIG BUSINESS

Ethel and Glenn Keller lost their business in a supermarket operation when Glenn had to move to Arizona to recuperate from an accident which paralyzed him from the waist down. In Arizona they needed to start all over to find a means of making a living.

Soon after they moved west Ethel started making cake icings for her new neighbors. Her reputation spread rapidly. In a short time she had a going neighborhood cake decorating business. Then when her friends learned she had a teaching certificate, they got a class together and paid her to teach the art of cake decorating.

Glenn regained the use of his legs in Arizona and took a job with a lumber company while Ethel started selling wedding cakes to supplement their income. Her sales soon grew to such a volume they decided to go into that business full time. The Kellers made plans to operate out of their home but were stopped because of zoning and had to rent a special hall, later investing in their own building.

At first Ethel handled the business on her own until a car accident put her temporarily in a wheelchair and Glenn had to quit his job to take over the operation. Later, when Ethel became active again, he did the baking while she put all her efforts into cake decorations and teaching.

A minister friend needed a chapel for his church services, so their daughter, Kathy, persuaded the Kellers to add a chapel to the building for a twofold purpose. It gave the minister a sanctuary for his services and provided them with a wedding chapel. Since then they have added complete photography services and flower arrangements as well as a bridal room where plans are made for the wedding. They also still have their original cake decorating school with a wholesale-retail supply center. In addition to the services offered on their premises, they cater weddings throughout the community.

Today they have a $140,000 annual business with twelve employees handling everything for weddings from the invitations to the reception. The whole family, including their three daughters Kathy, Hermeen and Margie, take an active part in the business.

PREPARING LUNCHES FOR OFFICE WORKERS

Sue and Charles H. in Chicago, Illinois started bringing delicious homemade submarine sandwiches to work for their own lunches. These sandwiches looked so appetizing other workers wanted them, so the sandwich makers began taking orders from two or three friends, charging $1 for each order.

In a short time workers throughout the entire office building knew of these special sandwiches and began ordering until the intake was as much as $50 or $60 every day.

Ina and Bill R. started a full-plate lunch program for office workers. They canvassed workers in a building and offered a choice of two types: an economy plate for $1.35 and a luxury lunch for $2. They, too, built a profitable business, making from $1,000 to $2,000 a month.

This is a needed service and should offer a wide open market to the innovative cook, because most of us who work away from home all day grow weary of the usual restaurant meal.

It would be necessary to check out local laws in your area before starting such a business. There may be health regulations with which you must comply as well as special licensing requirements. However, the need is great, customers are plentiful and most obstacles can be overcome. It could take a little time to handle the necessary details, but the results may well be worth the effort.

A WHOLE NEW APPROACH TO CATERING SERVICES

Conventional parties with good food, properly served, are always acceptable, but most of us would like to do something out of the ordinary if we could. Time limitations and lack of know-how keep the average party-giver in the same old rut following standard procedures, however. When someone does give an unusual party, that event is the talk of the town for months to come and its host or hostess the envy of friends and acquaintances.

Here is where an enterprising caterer can step into the picture and make a fortune specializing in theme parties and handling details such as invitations, decorations and food.

There are always such parties at specific times of year—Christmas, New Years Eve, Valentine's Day, St. Patrick's Day and others—but why not develop themes for every occasion?

If someone is going on a trip or has just returned, a travel party can be planned, with invitations resembling a travel agency folder and decorations depicting the vacation spot. The food could be a typical dish from the place being visited.

A party can be planned around the particular occupation of the guest of honor or a special project in which a group of people is involved. The list can be as long as your own imagination, and you need to promote the idea to all the people who give parties frequently. Read the society pages for names, and prepare attractive literature to describe your speciality.

Select a name for your service that depicts the theme party approach and advertise in good taste where it will mean the most. Better yet, offer to set up a party without charge for one of the most prominent party-givers in your community to demonstrate your ability to all the guests—your prospective customers for the future.

OFFERING SOMETHING NEW IN HOMEMADE FROZEN DINNERS

Olive P. is a widow who lives alone and loves to cook. She had no one to cook for—until she discovered a way to do what she loves and make money in the process.

She scrounged her neighborhood for empty TV dinner trays. She sterilized these thoroughly and stacked them for refilling. Then she started cooking. One day she prepared special roast beef and assembled some TV dinners. These she took around to her neighbors. On other days she made pork roast, chicken, meat loaf and turkey with dressing along with such extras as vegetables, applesauce and banana bread. She covered these homemade TV dinners with foil, marking the description on a piece of masking tape placed on each plate.

After her first week of free dinners, her neighbors began offering to pay for more. So Olive began taking special orders and selling these dinners. Soon she had all the customers she could handle.

Her investment was small since she didn't purchase the food until receiving the orders, and her customers paid her in advance. Rather than make an actual charge she let her customers give her whatever amount they felt was right, and she made from $2 to $3 a plate clearing about $30 a day working only part time.

This is an excellent business for any man or woman who likes to cook and is expert in the field. It might be good to give your first dinners to a few people who have lots of friends who will spread the word around. Just about anybody would prefer a special homemade frozen TV dinner—if it's good—to the usual commercial ones on the market. If you've got the talent, the market is waiting for you.

PREPARING SPECIAL MEALS FOR SINGLE PEOPLE

Most single people who live alone lose their interest in cooking because it's not much fun to cook for one person. There was a time when I thoroughly enjoyed cooking for my family and for guests, but now, after years of living alone, I have almost forgotten the art, and my busy schedule doesn't allow me time to revive it.

But we all have friends and would like to entertain in our own homes some of the time. Here lies a ready-made business for a good cook. If you enjoy cooking as Olive P. does, you can develop a productive operation by preparing guest meals for single men and women and for busy people in general.

You can easily develop a customer list through the local singles clubs, in special living quarters for singles and in publications for singles. In fact, a simple ad in the classified section should bring enough customers for a start, and word-of-mouth advertising will take over from there if your product is good.

An area in which single people seem to be totally neglected is that of frozen foods. I am sure an enterprising cook can develop a sizeable market for these products packaged in single portions. I have looked unsuccessfully in store after store for single portions of frozen vegetables. There are plenty of customers for boil-in-the-bag casserole dishes and different kinds of vegetables—all packaged separately for individual consumption.

SALES OUTLETS FOR FAVORITE RECIPES

Sit down and write a basic letter, preferably on a printed letterhead, with your name and address. Have 300 copies run off by an offset printer. Send this letter to famous people, local and national.

The letter should state that you are a freelance food columnist and would like to include this person in one of your columns. Ask each one to send you an eight-by-ten inch glossy personal photograph with favorite recipes or foods written on the back.

It is a good idea to print, also, a one-page questionnaire for more information about each individual. This you can use for an article which can be offered to magazines and newspapers along with the recipes.

Establish yourself with local weeklies having good circulation as Bev Barney did. You will receive more answers from celebrities if you mention the number of readers reached by your column. If you do not have such a connection and must operate on a strictly freelance basis, then your main asset will be persistence. Send a lot of letters and keep sending them even though the number of answers is small.

With a good collection of recipes from celebrities, you can sell to magazines and put out salable recipe books and pamphlets as well.

Obtain the names and addresses of various food organizations such as the Coffee Brewing Institute, Glassware Institute, Louisiana Yam Commission and National Broiler Council in your local library. Write to these organizations about your project, column, book or pamphlet. Tell them exactly what you want, and they will bend over backwards to help. You can get all kinds of photographs and information: let them know if you want color transparencies or black and white photographs. This will enable you to put together material for newspaper and magazine columns. It can be especially valuable in putting together specialized books—for children, for bachelors, for special diets or whatever your own creative imagination dictates to you.

This could easily lead to a syndicated newspaper column with several papers, throughout the country, carrying your columns simultaneously, each paying a fee for its use.

All this material will be invaluable to you, too, for numerous small sales to national magazines. Specialized periodicals for women, men, families or food products audiences usually buy recipes. You can find all or most of them in your library. Browse through these publications and gear your recipes to their subject matter.

PROVIDING A UNIQUE HOME-DELIVERED MEAL SERVICE

There are many people living alone who aren't eating properly either because they are no longer capable of cooking a balanced meal or because they have lost the incentive to do so.

These people are ready customers for a special home-delivered meal service which can be started on a small scale and developed into a big operation.

In the beginning, if you don't have the capital to invest in a refrigerated truck, you can deliver in a station wagon, small truck or even a passenger car as Fran R. did to neighbors in the senior citizen community where she lived. Her investment was minimal because she bought only what she needed for each order, and she earned about $200 as supplement to Social Security. Such meals can be cooked in the kitchen, wrapped in foil and delivered. They should be placed in a suitable plate for quick reheating in the oven when necessary.

The service is welcomed by invalids, senior citizens, people living alone and just busy people. You will need to offer well balanced food, attractively and tastefully prepared, with a great deal of variety from day to day. Promotion can be through convalescent homes, hospitals, senior citizens' clubs, neighborhood papers and personal contacts.

As your business develops, it would be well to put most of the proceeds, if not all, back into the business until you have reached a point where you can invest in a truck equipped with heating and refrigeration to protect the food for longer periods.

This business can be expanded from individual home services to mass deliveries to hospitals, industrial plants, special agencies, cafeterias and almost any place where quick food service is desired. But the personalized home delivery service is the most negelected and needed area. The competition should be little or none there, for the potential has barely been recognized.

TEACHING SPECIAL COOKING SECRETS

Anyone can become a cooking expert if they read and absorb the material available to them, but many people find it more satisfactory and pleasant to see the written material demonstrated. This opens the door to an excellent opportunity for teaching cookery, especially if you have some new hints to offer.

Teaching prospective cooks the usual routine material won't be enough to develop a thriving business. What you must offer is the unusual—information which is more difficult to acquire—and you will need to do some extensive research to uncover this.

Some of the recipes grandmother used to make have long been forgotten, but could be revived today. Go to your library and dig up some of those ancient cookbooks. See what "new" material you can gather there too.

If you are following my earlier suggestion and writing to celebrities for recipes, ask them for shortcuts they have discovered and suggestions for budgeting time and money.

Write to food manufacturers and distributors—there are lists of every business category in the library—and discover all you can about their products. Check your supermarkets and health food stores for names of food substitute manufacturers.

You can, after gathering this extensive information, organize a home economics class in your home. Promote the idea to office workers, students, to newly married couples whose names you can find on the society pages of your newspaper and to everyone that might want to learn something new about cooking.

A department store in Japan offered a special cooking class for men only. It proved so successful they had a long waiting list of prospective students.

This is a unique idea worth exploring when you consider all the bachelors and widowers living alone as well as husbands and wives with different working hours. It can be done easily in your own kitchen with no additional equipment as long as you limit the number of students per class.

Cooking is a popular art that many people wish to learn. The demand for information on this subject is so great that cooking demonstrations are featured on several television programs. A good home economist has an excellent opportunity to move into the professional field of TV demonstrations.

COOKING DEMONSTRATOR BECOMES TV PERSONALITY

The stories of many successful people sound as if these people were merely in the right place at the right time. This is often true, but a lot of preparation went ahead of that so-called "big break" at a specific time.

Rita Davenport is a good example of this. She was in the right place at the right time to be hired as hostess-producer of "Open House with Rita Davenport" on KPHO-TV in Phoenix, Arizona. But it wouldn't have done her much good to be there if she hadn't prepared herself for the opportunity.

She worked her way through college doing everything from cake decorating to performing as a dummy mannequin. This latter job required that she stand perfectly motionless. She did this so well that occasional observers were embarrassed when the dummy moved as they started to unfasten some of her wearing apparel.

When Rita graduated from college she worked at a variety of jobs which gained invaluable experience for her present work: she was a social worker, a model and finally a home economist for a public service company. It was in this position that she began doing special cooking demonstrations for the company on television. She did them so well that she was offered the job of handling the show itself when the opportunity arose.

Rita's knowledge of food and its preparation and her ability to demonstrate it to others publicly opened the door to a whole new career in television for her. Today she is not only well known for her own television show, but also does commercials for products and services that are carried on all the local TV stations.

This type of work often starts as a part-time opportunity. Sometimes, in the beginning, it offers little remuneration, but if it is what you want, it's worth the sacrifice. There are many opportunities for anyone capable of demonstrating special food preparation. The chances to do this on TV are especially abundant in communities served by cable television.

If the field interests you, explore the possibilities in your locality. You may discover either a new profession for yourself or a better way to promote your product.

PROVIDING AN UNUSUAL SPECIAL EVENTS SERVICE

Sumiko K., a Japanese woman, was stranded in the United States after her American husband's death with three small children to support and only a meager knowledge of the English language. She had to find a means of earning a living. Realizing that her only talent was cooking Japanese food, she worked out a way to turn this seeming limitation into an asset.

Sumiko secured names of girls soon to be married from the local newspaper society page and telephoned the parents of one of them. She told the girl's mother she would like to cook Japanese food which she would deliver personally to a shower party to be given for the engaged girl. To relieve the mother of any anxiety as to the quality of the food Sumiko agreed to cook a Japanese meal for five people. She said she would personally deliver it to the girl's home the next afternoon in time for their evening dinner. She also agreed to do this without charge.

The delicious dinner resulted in a commission to Sumiko to prepare food for twenty people attending the shower. Sumiko served the meal dressed in a Japanese kimono.

The food, prepared and delivered, cost Sumiko approximately $20. When asked what her charge was she didn't know what to say, but was delightfully surprised to receive a check for $100 from the girl's mother.

Word soon got around. Sumiko's home business expanded to a point where she had almost more parties than she could find the time to serve. A friend of mine said the last time he spoke with her that she was planning to handle a party of 1,500 people.

You may not have a speciality such as Sumiko had, but if you are a good cook, you can easily develop one. There are numerous cookbooks featuring recipes from other countries. Why not set yourself up as a specialist in this field, serving weddings and other special event parties with foreign dishes. If you wish, you can add a colorful touch, as Sumiko did, by dressing in the costume of countries whose food you are featuring.

SECRETS TO OBTAINING FREE ADVERTISING

Arts and crafts fairs have gained in popularity in the last few years, proving quite productive for the artists and the promoters. A food fair should be equally successful. It has been tried in a number of different ways with the measure of success depending largely on the method of handling.

A food fair is rather a big undertaking but an exciting one all the same. Some special fair promoters make as much or more at these fairs selling their own products as they do from other exhibitors.

No investment is needed if you have a sufficient number of food merchants purchasing booth space. The exhibitors handle all the details of their individual booths and pay the costs involved. The income from their space rentals should more than cover any expense you would have for your own displays.

The biggest thing you would offer your exhibitors is publicity. If you plan your fair around an interesting theme and secure exhibitors with exciting and innovative food products, you should have no trouble interesting newspaper, TV and radio people in covering the event.

An ideal location for such a fair is in a popular shopping center where your customers are already present. Such a location will also give you added advertising and publicity for the event at no cost to you. Sylvia J. sponsored a fair in a local shopping center, clearing $1,500 in two days from exhibitor fees plus the sales of her own candies (made with recipes of other countries).

You may not be ready for such a huge promotional idea as this, but there are many other ways to secure free advertising. If your product is unique, your service out of the ordinary and your story interesting, the daily and weekly newspapers will very likely consider doing a story on your project. Get a public relations friend to approach them for you. Contact radio and television stations too, particularly those with interview programs. If there is a food demonstration program on one of your local television stations, that will be your best possibility.

THREE IMPORTANT RULES FOR A
SUCCESSFUL FOOD-MAKING PROJECT

1. Develop a recipe that is distinctly different and appealing in taste and appearance.

This can be one of your own recipes developed in your kitchen, one that you have discovered through contacts with other cooks or prominent people, or one which you were able to improve from a recipe you found in a good cook book.

2. Choose a type of food that has popular appeal. Some kinds of food are generally more popular than others, and a recipe using some of these ingredients has more assurance of immediate acceptance.

3. Promote your product through every possible media.

Look over this chapter carefully and refresh your memory on the means others have used successfully. Give your own product all the push you can muster; never skimp on promotion.

7

Unlimited Opportunities
for Specialized Handwork

Styles in wearing apparel, home furnishings, accessories and even children's toys are constantly changing. The desire most people have to keep up with the latest trends offers a never-ending opportunity for the artist who is handy with a needle and thread. The expert seamstress or tailor is never without work, and in most cases has more prospective customers than there is time to handle. The secret is in word-of-mouth recommendation.

A tenant in one of my apartments, Dick L., came to our city without knowing anyone there. He took over a small tailor shop in a cubbyhole behind a downtown newsstand, sharing it with a cleaning establishment. The cleaners jobbed out all their work since there was no space for actual cleaning, but the two businesses thrived almost from the start.

Dick was a first-rate tailor. He needed only a few customers in the beginning to show what he could do. From then on, he had all the customers he could handle. He got his first customers from people like us—his few acquaintances—and from strangers who were willing to give him a try when he offered them a price break they could hardly afford to turn down. All of us were happy to recommend his fine work to others.

He had no investment: the shop was equipped, and he worked on material and clothes purchased by his customers. His rent was only $60 a month and he made about $250 a week. His secret was starting on a small scale and letting the business pay for its own expansion.

CRAFTS PEOPLE WITH NEEDLE AND THREAD IN DEMAND

I have always had difficulty finding good seamstresses who

could make clothes for me inexpensively in a reasonable period of time. The same is true in a number of areas requiring the talents of handwork specialists. There are customers all around you waiting to find the craftsman who can offer custom-made accessories that are different. And there is a steady flow of business available to experts in draperies, curtains and upholstery from the new homes, apartment complexes, townhouses and condominiums. The field is wide open to the imaginative needlecraftsman or to those gifted in related arts.

HOW TO DISCOVER WHAT IS NEEDED AND WANTED

The secret is to match your skills with the need in your community. First you should assess your own abilities, listing every type of handwork you feel you can do with expert skill; then put together a questionnaire about the needs and desires for this handwork. Now canvass the areas where you would be most likely to find customers for your particular art. If you are skilled in dress-making or tailoring, office buildings are probably your best bet.

Tell each person you approach exactly what you are doing—that you are planning to start a business of this nature and you want to know what types of services are most needed and wanted. Let them know that you want, if possible, to offer the particular type of service he or she has been seeking. If you make each contact on a personal basis and indicate a genuine interest in serving the community according to its real needs, you should find people more than eager to cooperate.

Should you want to offer your services in the field of household furnishings, such as draperies or upholstery, then contact new homeowners. You can find these names in your local newspapers.

Specialized fields, such as wedding apparel, are easy to survey by merely watching the engagement announcements in the society section of the paper. The toy market could be explored through toy shops and toy department buyers. Gift shop owners, managers and department buyers would be able to furnish adequate information for salable gift merchandise.

PRODUCING A MARKETABLE PRODUCT

Run-of-the-mill merchandise is always available in almost any category. The secret of a successful product lies in the exceptional craftsmanship that makes the difference between a mediocre business and a highly successful operation. In the field of handwork there is an abundance of available second-rate merchandise and service, especially in this age of production versus quality.

Your success will come from offering something more. If you are prepared to deliver that something extra in custom-made clothing, drapes, upholstery, accessories, gift items or whatever your particular specialty, you can be sure you have a marketable product. This is definitely true if you have surveyed the market and found that what you are offering is needed and wanted.

Proper promotion and marketing is the next vital factor, for no matter how good the product or service, it won't be sold unless people know it is available. Discover your own best skills, uncover needs and desires, and then let the world know what you have to offer.

CUSTOM-MADE CLOTHES AT REASONABLE PRICES

The dressmaker who does an exceptional job with the customer's choice of material and pattern is much in demand and can develop a sizeable business. But the seamstress or tailor who can create individualized clothing that fits the customer's specific tastes and personality has the ultimate to offer.

SECRETARY DESIGNS CLOTHES

Gladys P. had done some fashion design work for a local department store and had always made her own clothes. Later, when she was working as a secretary, she began experimenting with custom-made clothes for herself. Soon her fellow workers started asking where she bought her clothes.

When she revealed her secret, they asked her to design and make clothes for them. In a few months she had enough customers to quit her job and go into full-time work as a custom dress designer. She charged $25 for the design and $15 for labor, making as much as $65 in a day. The customer bought the material. One of the secrets to her success was a little added personal touch. She put labels on each dress which read: "Made for _____."

If your talents include the ability to design clothes and select colors and material for a reasonable cost, you have a business potential that is unlimited. The secret to success in this field is the ability to match the clothing to the personalities, complexions and overall traits of your customers.

You would be wise to offer this type of service to a few friends in the beginning to prove your ability in the field both to yourself and to others. Then you can be assured of a highly successful and profitable business offering a service that many have hoped to find.

PROVIDING MENDING SERVICES BEYOND THE ORDINARY

I can still remember the day when I could take my clothes to the cleaners and know they would mend any little rips and sew on buttons that came off in cleaning. Today such service is quite beyond the ordinary. In fact, it is only a pleasant memory of an era long gone.

Clara W. decided to revive this long-lost service in her community, and in so doing has built herself a flourishing business which she operates out of her home.

She contacted several cleaning establishments in her vicinity and contracted to do this service for them, offering it on a 24-hour basis. Her husband works with her doing the pick-up and delivery; two of her daughters help with the sewing. They have all the work they can handle and keep sewing machines and needles going constantly to stay on top of the demand.

Clara started with a sewing machine she already owned so she had no initial investment. She bought additional equipment from the proceeds of the business. The business grew to a point where she could make as much as $15 an hour. Her secret was reviving a much-desired service and delivering it as promised.

MEN'S ALTERATIONS PROVIDE GOOD INCOME

John H. made arrangements to do alterations in a men's clothing shop. When in the course of his work customers would come to him wearing suits that needed buttons replaced, ripped linings repaired or other types of mending, he would offer to take care of these things. When his reputation for this extra service soon became known, people started coming to the store specifically for his services. This sideline developed into so much extra business that he hired an assistant. At the same time, the store gained several new customers.

He made from $100 to $200 extra a week charging from $7 to $10 a suit. The secret to his second-income success was in the special services he gave his customers while on the job.

RESTYLING OUTDATED CLOTHES

Changing styles cause us all to throw away items of clothing that frequently are barely worn. What a golden opportunity there is here for the ingenious seamstress or tailor who can turn these outdated clothes into modern styles!

I found someone who was able to style a pair of tight leg pants for me by inserting a triangular piece of black material in at the bottom of each leg. The suit was red, and the black inset gave the outfit a sharp and very "mod" appearance. That same old tight pant leg can be made into a smart new long dress by opening the crotch.

I have seen more than one mother change old clothing for their children—boys and girls alike—into model fashion items. But I don't know of any of these mothers who recognized the profit potential for doing this commercially. Some enterprising seamstresses have done it before, but certainly the field is open with plenty of customers available—once they know of the service.

If you are already doing this for yourself and family, you have ready-made samples of your work. Tell people about it and show them what you've done. It's a much-needed service—one I could have used a number of times.

OFFERING A NEW APPROACH TO CLOTHES ALTERATIONS

Most of the larger stores have alterations people on the spot to handle this type of work for a fee, but there are many small dress shops that don't.

Many times I have decided not to purchase a particular item of clothing in a smaller shop or in one of the low-cost department stores because the pants or dress needed shortening. I would have been delighted if, in any one or those stores, the clerk had handed me a card and said, "Call this number, and I am sure you can get the alterations done at a reasonable cost." I would have been especially happy if she had told me this alteration person would come to my home, do the fitting there and return my clothing to me at my house when the work was completed.

HOUSEWIFE DEVELOPED PROFITABLE ALTERATION BUSINESS

Terry L. offered to do alterations in her home for two small neighborhood dress shops, and in less than three months had all the customers she could handle. There was no investment necessary since she already had all the needed equipment in her home. Her advertising was all done by the store clerks and owners—she didn't even need to invest in business cards. Because her work was good, the business expanded to customers other than the store clientele, who were referred to her by those she served through these two stores. She made as much as $750 in a month.

The secret is to find some small clothing stores in your neighborhood and possibly a low-cost department store, so you won't have to travel great distances for most of the customers.

ALTERATION RELIEF LADY EARNS GOOD MONEY

Some of the larger stores already employing alteration people would welcome added help, because most of these alteration departments have a backlog of work and are unable to give immediate service. Paula B. did alteration work in her home for three department stores in a neighborhood shopping center, relieving their regular alteration people, and made $200 in a week. The secret to a profitable operation in this field is developing a regular business arrangement with a group of department stores located fairly close together. Before setting up such a business you can survey the stores in your neighborhood and arrive at a fairly good estimate of how much business you could anticipate.

OPERATING A CUSTOM-MADE DRAPERY SERVICE

Draperies are items for which the purchaser has to rely on the salesman to know what is needed and best suited to the situation. The customer can pick materials but cannot see the completed item until it is delivered. This puts a great deal of responsibility on the drapery shop operator or salesman, so it is important that anyone going into this business know the trade well.

There are no specialized schools where you can get his kind of training; the best way to learn the profession is by working for someone who has a good reputation in the field.

Quite a sizeable amount of money can be involved in the

purchase of draperies. Consequently, the customer wants to be certain that his or her product is going to be of the best quality.

HOW TO ESTABLISH YOUR REPUTATION

If you want to operate a custom-made drapery service from your home you would be wise to establish your reputation and reliability in the beginning. Since you will not have the advantage of the business front a store building offers, you will need to prove your expertise in other ways.

The best proof is an actual demonstration of what you can produce. You can do this by offering your services to friends and acquaintances as an introductory offer at reduced rates, or you may want to take on a job for some prominent family, with the understanding that the pay will be based on satisfaction. A few successes on this basis will establish your reputation adequately to give your business a firm foundation.

The secret to setting up a successful drapery business in your home with the least amount of risk is to start by working through a department store or other established source. Spend one day a week in the store taking orders to work on in your home.

LITTLE KNOWN FACTS ABOUT GIFT MAKING

In these days of affluence when so many people already have nearly everything, it is difficult to discover something new, but something old may seem novel today. Traditional needle art is in this category: anyone who is able to revive the art of some of the very old laces should find a whole new market in gift merchandise.

A newspaper column some time ago discussed the revival of Battenburg lace, which was popular in the Victorian era. It was made by basting braid to a tissue paper pattern and filling up the space in between the loops of braid with weaving.

Tablecloths trimmed with this lace are a perfect match for today's popular antique furniture items. Such tablecloths and other items trimmed with this lace bring top prices.

Woven wall hangings have gained considerable interest in recent years. The Eye of God (Ojo de Dios), which is said to bring good fortune wherever it hangs, has become a popular housewarming gift, especially in the Southwest. Much of its appeal is due to the fact that it has been inspired by increasingly popular Indian handicrafts.

HOUSEWIFE TURNS WEAVING INTO PROFITABLE OPERATION

Ellie J. never attempted craft work until she took up weaving as a hobby. As it took up more and more of her time and her house space (with five looms and 50 yarn storage bins), she felt a need to justify the cost and time. At this point she put her product on the market. Today not only are her wall hangings popular gift items for some of the finest homes in the city, but many of her unique art pieces are hanging in the larger business offices around town.

Her secret is a business that has no competition. The demand for her work grows every day, bringing her a far-above-average daily income.

The biggest expense for such a business is in the looms and the yarn. This varies with the size and number of looms. It is still possible to make more than double your cost on every sale.

MAKING STUFFED GIFT ITEMS FOR ALL AGES

Stuffed animals and dolls have always been popular sales items, and whenever something different in stuffed items is produced, it has even greater sales potential.

When my mother was confined to her bed for several months there was very little we could give her that she could enjoy. She couldn't see clearly or hear very well, but she could feel, and I looked everywhere for a soft stuffed animal that she could have in the bed with her. I finally found a small cat that looked somewhat like the Siamese she used to have. She held that cat in her hands most of the night and day. She wasn't senile, but only unable to communicate well because of weakness and speech difficulty, but she did seem to enjoy that soft padded animal. It was difficult to find, though, and I almost gave up the search before I located this one little stuffed cat.

An enterprising needle and thread artist who can come up with a variety of these soft, flexible stuffed animals and other items will have a ready market—especially if they are promoted for such purposes as this.

WIDOW SELLS STUFFED TOYS THROUGH GIFT SHOP

Stuffed items are popular as decorative pieces too, for a davenport or a bed. One of the cleverest stuffed items I have seen was an octopus made of a big swatch of material stuffed with cloth and tied off with string. Its legs were made of strips of yarn that completely covered the head and were then braided into eight long strips. Eyes, nose and mouth were sewed on its face and a bow was tied around its neck. Alice J., a widow in her mid-seventies, put these together and sold all she could make through a nearby gift shop. She said they were especially popular with adults.

She also made and sold bean bags in all shapes and sizes—frogs, cats, squares, circles—anything. Alice had a specialty item for babies which she called "Baby Doll." She used a gingerbread man cookie cutter as a guideline for cutting out the doll. She stuffed it with cloth instead of cotton to make it softer and more chewable, then put long legs and arms on it so the baby could grab it easily. It was easy to clean—could just be thrown in the washing machine. It sold well particularly for baby showers.

The cost of making these items can be kept to less than $1 by using scraps of material. The finished products sold for from $3 to $10.

Alice also took beat-up stuffed toys and ornaments, remade them into attractive pieces and sold them to the same outlet.

OPERATING A DOLL HOSPITAL AND CLOTHES SHOPPE

Jane C. started repairing and rebuilding old used dolls for a crippled children's hospital. She would wash the dolls and generally clean them up, style their hair, and then make a whole wardrobe of clothes for each doll. Some of her friends saw what a remarkable job she was doing with these dolls and talked her into doing the same things for their youngsters—only this time for a fee.

Jane's doll wardrobes were unique and caught on quickly. She set up one room in her large house just to display doll clothes. Her secret was making wardrobes to fit many of the best-selling dolls. These items soon had customers coming to her door—both young and old.

SPECIALTIES BRING BIG PROFITS

One of Jane's specialties was Barbie Doll wardrobes. She made everything for these dolls from swim suits to wedding clothes, using mostly scrap materials. The wardrobes sold for as much as $15.

Jane also developed a sizeable business dressing dolls in foreign costumes. To do this she studied the clothing of countries all over the world, making sure every item of her wardrobe was authentic. With each doll she sold she included an attractively printed folder containing information about the country represented. She got as much as $35 for some of these.

If you are handy with a needle and thread and have a flair for fashion, a doll shoppe set up to look much like a regular dress shop should make a very unique and profitable business for you. The original investment can be small. You can start with discarded dolls, scrap material and your own sewing machine.

MAKING UNUSUAL UTILITY ITEMS

There is always a good market for an item that is useful, and attractive and that features something extra.

Velma H. needed to earn extra money but couldn't leave her home because she had small children to take care of. One rainy day she was distressed by a puddle left on her floor from the dripping umbrellas of two visitors. She decided to do something about it.

Velma began working on a way to cover folded umbrellas and keep them from dripping. She designed a simple plastic sleeve which cost only a few cents to make. In the beginning she made these only for friends, but then decided it might be a welcome item for business places. She made samples and mailed these to a number of businesses. In a short time her mail box was flooded with orders. The low cost of these items enabled businesses to print their names on them and give them away for advertising purposes.

If you live in a part of the country where there is a lot of rain you might want to explore the possibilities of making and selling umbrella sleeves.

TURNING OTHER UTILITY ITEMS INTO PROFIT

There probably are a number of utility items you are already making or using. Take a look at these and see what you can do to make them a little different and, possibly, more useful.

Coat hangers that prevent clothes from slipping are always desirable. The most attractive ones I have seen are covered with strips of ruffled net in various colors. Clothes brushes and scouring pads made from this same netting material are equally popular, as are ceiling brushes. Covers for appliances, pot holders and mitts all offer opportunities for the innovative person to improve upon.

Utility aprons with large pockets all around the bottom are not always available in stores and should always be popular items because they are both practical and attractive.

If you can find these and other clever items at a church bazaar, why not in a commercial shop as well? Check your own homes and those of friends and see what is needed and wanted. The pin cushion made over a partially opened tuna fish can, the dolls that cover the brush end of a broom, scissor holders that look like a lady's old fashioned boot and knit or velvet coat hangers could all be developed and marketed.

MAKING ACCESSORIES WITH UNIQUE APPEAL

Veronica B., while living in a wooded area, began making buttons from wood and from elk or deer horns. She was an artisan who saw a potential in the secluded area where she lived and made the best of it. She didn't have to buy material—all she had to do was walk outside her home and pick it off the ground.

She designed the buttons completely on her own with no pattern or designs from a book, and she says they came out perfectly on her first try. Since there was no electricity in her home, she had to slice the horns with a hacksaw in the beginning. Later, when she moved, she was able to use an electric saw.

The variations in color in her buttons is from the natural variation in the horns themselves. She used no added coloring.

She also fashioned buttons from several types of wood—ironwood, pyracantha, cedar, madrone and mesquite. In addition to a wide variety of buttons she also made earrings and pendants from horn and different kinds of wood. The secret to the popular appeal of these products was in their unique characteristics.

There are as many opportunities to develop unique accessories as there are items themselves. Macramé belts and purses are very popular. Handmade purses that combine utility and attractiveness are always in demand.

Look at your own surroundings to see what you may have been overlooking. You may have a gold mine in your own environment just as a California housewife did in her front yard.

UNREVEALED KNITTING POTENTIAL FOR MEN AND WOMEN

Ralph P. had a severe case of arthritis in his hands and needed to find a means of exercising them. He took up knitting as therapy and discovered it was a fascinating craft. In a short time he found that there were all kinds of wearing apparel and a variety of other items he could knit. To cut costs, he went to Goodwill and other such outlets to secure old sweaters which he ripped up for the yarn.

His pleasure in this new craft was so evident that his wife became interested too. Soon they were both involved in a number of knitting projects. At first they made things only for fun and therapy, but as others saw the results of their work, the merchandise began to sell. Eventually, they went into a custom-made knitting operation. Word-of-mouth advertising combined with the quality of their work brought them customers from all over. They now have all the business they want, making from $250 to $300 a month working part time.

Ralph feels that many men are missing out on a very satisfying occupation when they think knitting is for women only. He has found it not only profitable and healthy but delightfully pleasant as well.

The secret to more extensive merchandising in this area is producing a better-than-average product and making a real effort to promote it.

STARTING YOUR OWN DRESSMAKING SHOP

Sara L. had two extra rooms in her home, which was in an area already zoned for business. She and her friend, Lela J., decided to set up a custom tennis dressmaking shop. They turned one of the rooms into a display area.

Their customers were invited to pick out their own material, pattern and trim. The shop would then buy this from them and make the dress, shorts or whatever tennis apparel is desired. If the customer liked the results she could buy it; if not, Sara and Lela kept it, putting it on display and selling it to another customer.

Both women were good seamstresses and could turn out a dress or outfit quickly. They were also creative and inventive, and could make these dresses and outfits economically, giving their customers more for their money—better handmade quality at reasonable cost.

They used Sara's daughter and granddaughter as models. The shop operators have also set up a rather unique sales plan, giving one dress free to anyone who secures a new customer for them. In addition to tennis dresses they make tennis shorts, skirts and bloomers. Most of these cost them less than $5 to make and sell for $15 to $20 each. Their secret is selling a sports attire specialty in a part of the country where sports go on the whole year round.

CUSTOM SUIT SHOP

Gus and Sue P. operate a custom suit shop for men and women in a California town. They have samples for their customers to choose from, or will make whatever style is desired. A customer can save money by bringing his or her own material. If takes four or five days to get a suit after it is ordered. For their investment of $2,000 they can make as much as $300 in a week.

PROVIDING A CUSTOMIZED UPHOLSTERY
AND CHAIR COVER SERVICE

Ken R. worked in a grocery store warehouse and as a liquor store clerk. He did upholstery work on the side for friends and acquaintances. When his reputation spread far beyond friends and acquaintances, he built a large enough following to borrow money and buy out an upholstery shop.

His business has increased to a point now where there are many prospective customers waiting for his services. In fact, I first learned about him through a friend who has been trying to get in touch with him. She and her husband had heard such excellent reports of his work they are willing to wait, if necessary, to secure his services. Quality work is the secret to his success.

BUSINESS CAN BE STARTED ON SMALL SCALE

Ken says an upholsterer can start this business in a small way with an investment of approximately $1,500. The most important piece of equipment is a heavy-duty sewing machine. A good used one can be purchased for $500 or $600. You will also need paint for refinishing the wood on the furniture, an air staple gun, a drill, a tack strip, hand needles and a regulator which is like an ice pick. You will want horses on which to set the furniture you are covering, regular cord and welt cord, hog rings, hog ring pliers and diagonal hand stapler.

It isn't necessary to stock material: you can take orders from sample books and buy material as you sell a job.

Ken says there is more money in furniture upholstering than in car upholstery, but the car upholstery is much easier and quicker. It is possible to make anywhere from $1,000 to $2,000 a month in this business.

SELDOM USED APPROACHES TO DISCOVER NEW OPPORTUNITIES

Most of us are inclined to look far off into the distance for the end of the rainbow where we hope a pot of gold lies waiting. Too frequently, we are looking right over that pot of gold sitting so close we could reach out and touch it. There are some excellent examples in this chapter of people who did remember to look for something close at hand. These people found the secrets to discovering pots of gold. They found them in custom-made clothing, a weaving hobby, doll wardrobes for crippled children, buttons from natural materials, knitting for something more than therapy and on a rainy day. The best sources are often those that you can reach today—not something far away in distance and time.

Begin now to check your own potential capabilities, the facilities around your house and yard and the neighborhood in which you live. There are opportunities waiting for everyone. It's a matter of seeing them from where you stand now.

8

Second-Income Opportunities
for the Versatile Worker

In this day of specialists, the man or woman who can do a lot of jobs well is in great demand, as is the competent craftsman who will do the smaller jobs so often needed around a home or business. This means that the opportunities are unlimited for the versatile worker in home crafts who makes his or her talents known. It is an excellent field with a secret advantage—it enables the worker to start a sideline business that can grow to whatever size you want. The necessary skills are often developed through doing this kind of work for yourself in your own home.

Lucy P. had a knack for inside house painting and tile laying. When she and her husband bought an old rundown house, Lucy made it into one of the neighborhood showplaces by painting the interior, putting up some paneling, papering the walls in a couple of rooms and tiling the floors in the front foyer and one other room. Her friends were so impressed that some of them persuaded her to redo parts of their homes. Soon she had a part-time business going, making a couple of hundred dollars for two or three days' work a week. She had no investment since her friends paid in advance for the material. Later, when she expanded her business, she had accumulated enough capital to purchase material by the job.

SECRETS FOR TURNING SHORT HOURS INTO GOOD PAY

Quality workmanship by skilled craftsmen is the secret in making top money; the person who knows his job so thoroughly that he can perform it well without unnecessary time delays can make good money working short hours.

George J. was a carpenter for several years. Through careful observation, he learned another trade which paid well. He helped lay bricks when working with experts in this field, and gradually developed a special talent for the craft. He continued to use this skill over the years, doing jobs on the side in addition to his regular job. As his reputation grew, his customer list increased, and he decided to give up the salaried job and devote all his time to small bricklaying jobs. Now he does brick work for patios, fences, flower boxes, and other small areas, making $300 to $450 a week working half days. He can easily double that if he wants to work longer hours, but working part time gives him an adequate income with more free time for leisure activities. This business can be started with $100 or less.

HOW TO LEARN THE CRAFT

George says bricklaying isn't a difficult craft to learn. The secret of developing the skill is to get a job as helper for an expert bricklayer and apply yourself to learning the technique. This doesn't take long, and it provides an excellent means for making good money working as many or as few hours as you wish.

This is true of many crafts. If you learn the skills thoroughly and apply what you learn, it is possible to make better-than-average pay working just a few hours a week.

NEW APPROACHES TO MAKING GOOD MONEY DOING ODD JOBS

Steve K. was a janitor in a high school for 11 years, then a community worker and special counselor for three years. During this period he earned considerable extra money working at odd jobs and developed top skills in a wide variety of fields.

He gained such as excellent reputation as a versatile craftsman that he retired early from his salaried position and started doing odd jobs on a full-time basis. Steve had learned many different crafts when he owned rentals and couldn't afford hiring someone to do the work for him. Out of necessity he became a first-class craftsman in practically every phase of house repair and upkeep. His one speciality was doing everything necessary to keep a home in shape.

DEVELOPING CUSTOMERS

He developed his present business by first doing one job for a customer, making sure his work was satisfactory before even presenting a bill. Then often he was asked to do another odd job for that same customer—sometimes three or four different things before he was through.

His main emphasis then was—and still is—a satisfied customer. His secret is that he makes sure that everyone for whom he does a job is satisfied. Steve goes over every phase of the work with each person who employs him. Together they check out all details to be certain the work has been done as ordered—BEFORE he presents the bill.

His jobs include painting, paneling, installing counter tops in kitchens, installing and repairing plumbing fixtures, minor carpentry work, window installations, cooler service, roofing repair and practically everything to do with house repair and upkeep.

It is possible to make from $800 to $1,000 a month in this field working without strain. It all depends on the ability and the character of the craftsmen.

HOW TO START

To start a business doing odd jobs in house repair and upkeep it is essential to have a good used pickup truck. Steve says it is important that it be a reliable truck for, to be successful in this field, you must be dependable—which means being on the job when you say you will be there, not an hour or even 30 minutes later. Good transportation is essential for getting to a job on time. The truck, which can usually be purchased on time payments, will cost $500 or $600, and additional equipment will run in the neighborhood of $500. You will need a circular saw, heavy-duty drill, saber saw, electric planer, many screwdrivers, wood and metal chisels, paint brushes and rollers, other painting equipment, all kinds of screws and bolts, and a good tool box to safeguard these tools.

Steve doesn't keep many supplies on hand: it is an easy matter to purchase these for each individual job.

PROVIDING A SELDOM FOUND REPAIR SERVICE

There are always jobs around a home that the man of the house never finds time to do. How nice it would be to have a handy repair man or woman come to the door at regular times and ask if you have any small appliances that need repairing!

Having a camper would be the best way to start this type of service, but it can be started very easily from the trunk of your car. Jules L. began this way. He went door to door in his own subdivision and found numerous customers who had broken-down lamps, stuck drawers, damaged furniture, toys and other small items that needed repair. Most of these he was able to fix on the spot, and he made close to $50 the first day.

HANDYMAN DEVELOPED BIG PAY BUSINESS
THROUGH SPECIAL ADVERTISING

Gale J. increased his income by doing odd jobs on the side. He had worked in a variety of crafts. This qualified him to handle many different kinds of jobs as an all-around handyman.

His secret? He used one simple slogan: WE DO EVERYTHING. He incorporated this into all his advertising, in the classified section of the newspaper, in handbills and on business cards.

Within a three-month period he was getting so many calls that he had to hire others to help him, and soon he gave up his regular job going into a full-time business operation.

His jobs ranged from repairing a leak in the kitchen sink to filling a hole in somebody's back yard. He had to invest very little since he had most of the necessary tools for his own personal use. These could be purchased for $300 to $500, or considerably less if you hire out jobs in the beginning for which you don't have equipment. He makes as much as $75 to $100 a day. He attributes his success to his simple slogan and his ability to live up to it.

"If I don't have anyone on hand who can do the job," he said, "I find someone to do it. I never turn down a job. I can't with that kind of advertising."

REPAIRING SMALL APPLIANCES

There are many repair shops for the larger appliances. Small appliances such as toasters, percolators and mixers are often repaired through the manufacturer. The problem with this is usually the time element. Most people don't want to be without those items for so long. Jack J. discovered this several years ago when he started tinkering with small appliances for a few of his friends. The first thing he knew, more and more people were asking him to fix their small appliances. He soon had a business going for himself.

In the army he had gained considerable experience in electrical repair and had, in fact, passed tests indicating a specific aptitude in this field. Nevertheless, he wanted to be certain of his knowledge, so he got all the information he could from the manufacturers of small appliances. Later he opened a small shop specializing entirely in repairing these items. That was several years ago. Now his business location has grown from one tiny room to a large plant with a dozen employees working under him. Customers come to him from all over the city rather than deal with manufacturers. His secret was fast and efficient service no matter how small the job.

He says such a business can be started on a small scale for about $500. It is advisable to stock parts for the best known appliances, but it is not difficult to secure parts for other items from manufacturers when necessary.

It is possible to make $2,000 a month or more if you are located where there isn't too much competition. Word-of-mouth advertising from satisfied customers has been his greatest asset.

HOW TO BECOME A FURNITURE DOCTOR

The best ways to find customers for furniture repair work are going door to door or placing classified ads in the paper. Going door to door is the secret to securing customers because you can solicit each repair customer face to face. A lot of people won't bother to take something into a shop; instead they put it aside and do nothing about it. It is much easier to get it repaired if someone is at your door offering to fix it.

A small furniture sales shop evolved out of the repair business which Ben K. started in his garage. He went door to door and found all the customers he needed as well as several persons who just wanted to get rid of their worn-out furniture items. He restored these to a nearly-new condition and sold them in his furniture shop. He does a thriving business in both furniture repair and sales.

Ben had no investment in the beginning. He used the earnings from his repair business to start his sales shop. His only expense there was for utilities, a few tools, paints and varnish—less than $200. He cleared as much as $2,000 in a month.

PAINTING FURNITURE PROFITABLE PASTIME

Erma K., a housewife, located hard-to-sell items in furniture stores and offered to paint designs on them, giving them a hand-painted appearance. The stores paid her the difference between what they would have sold for before and what they got for them after she had given them her special touch. She has made as much as $150 a week this way, working just a few hours.

This same woman takes mis-matched pieces of furniture from used furniture stores, auctions and even from alleys where they have been discarded. She paints these pieces to match, making them into sets.

She can make as much as $300 a week, and her initial investment was near to nothing. She calls herself "The Furniture Doctor," but she does both repair work and furniture sales. The two go hand in hand.

OPERATING A REPAIR SHOP FOR SANTA

In many cities around the country you will find thriving "Christmas Shops" during the holiday season. I discovered that many persons use this method for starting a year-round shop for stationery, greeting cards, gift wrappings and small gift items. During the holidays they specialize in these same things along with special Christmas letter service, tree ornaments, lights, holiday trimmings and all the little extras needed at Christmas time. These shops usually draw large crowds of customers during the holiday period and establish a customer following at this time which they can keep in the year-round shop if they offer the same type of service.

The same should be true of a Repair Shop for Santa, geared to making old toys new. Examples of expertise in this field should be prominently displayed. There are families that find it difficult to buy the kind of new toys they want to give their youngsters each year. This theme lends itself to a unique store front and interior design that will automatically draw people to it during the holiday season. If you handle your promotion properly and offer to make old toys new at lower-than-new prices, you can build an excellent clientele.

This can easily be transformed into a year-round toy repair shop. You can actually keep the Santa theme all year if you wish. A Christmas shop in California does this and has a good year-round business, making as much as $1,500 in a month. They never change the name—it is always "The Christmas Shop." You might want to consider doing it the same way for a Santa's Repair Shop.

HOUSE PAINTER REVEALS SECRETS TO HIS SUCCESS

Franklin Rogers started painting by working with his brother-in-law when he was 18 years old. He worked in a shoe repair shop six days a week and painted on the seventh day, learning the trade by doing it. During the war he did painting work under a journeyman contractor to complete his apprenticeship.

"Without some type of expert instruction," Rogers said, "it is difficult to learn all angles of painting. The union requires three years, and a painter isn't worth much to a contractor his first six months."

Rogers later worked for a period of time under another painting contractor. During this time he started getting painting opportunities here and there on the side. If the job was for the neighbor next door to the contractor's customer, however, Franklin wouldn't take that job. He felt it belonged to the contractor. He took only those that had absolutely no connection with the contractor.

Word-of-mouth advertising—the only kind he has ever had—brought him more and more customers until he built a sizeable business on the side. It was then he decided to go into business for himself.

The secret to his success in this field is due largely to his work philosophy. "If you try hard enough, you can please most people," he says. "If you promise something, your word should be as good as your bond. If your words are no good, what good is a written guarantee?"

Rogers says you can start in this business with as little as $1500 or $2000 if your credit is good; you can finance each job as you get it. You will need to borrow from $100 to $150 to handle each work project. The secret here is paying that loan back immediately when you get paid. You can borrow again as many times as you need to as long as you continue to pay each loan back immediately upon receipt of your payment from the customer.

To start, you will need drop cloths, ladders, brushes and a pickup truck. An apprentice makes about $4 an hour; this is more than doubled when you become a full-fledged painter.

PROVIDING A CLEANING SERVICE FOR HOME OR OFFICE

This is an excellent field to start as a sideline, especially if you specialize in office buildings which are always cleaned at night. You can still handle a daytime job while you build up your cleaning business and find time for sleeping, too, if you plan your time well.

Harry T., a disabled veteran, worked with another cleaning firm for a period of time, learning the business and establishing a reputation for himself. Then he went out an; solicited business on his own. Now he has a very successful business operation. His secret is satisfied customers. One good job leads to another as the word gets around. He has built his business largely through recommendations from his customers.

It takes about $700 to start a business of this kind. You will need a buffer, mop, mop bucket, gear press, dust cloths, sponges, dry mop, vacuum, wax and soap. A man and woman working together as a team six or seven hours five nights a week can make $1,000 a month.

SERVICING LAWNS AND GARDENS

A lawn maintenance service is often started on a small scale but can develop into a very expansive business. It is a field where work is nearly always available for the conscientious worker who is willing to go out after it.

Lawn and garden maintenance offers opportunities for people of all ages. In recent years a number of retirees who have gone into this field to supplement their incomes found it far better than a supplement. Both men and women are doing it successfully; frequently a whole family or a father and his sons handle the work.

BUILDING A BUSINESS BY DEMONSTRATION

This is the case with Melvin L. Johnson. He was tired of the nervous tension and strain of working as manager of a service station. As a young boy he had worked with his father doing yard maintenance. He always enjoyed the work so decided to go back into that field.

He had cards printed, and his two sons distributed these cards throughout the neighborhood, leaving them in mailboxes. Soon they began to get calls for work. As they worked in a neighborhood and demonstrated the quality of their work, others would approach them to do their yards. The business grew rapidly.

Required equipment includes a lawnmower, edger, hand clippers, rakes, brooms, fertilizer, extra gas for the mower and a pickup truck. It is possible, with used equipment, to start the business on a small scale with approximately $1,000. As money starts coming in you can begin to increase the amount and quality of your equipment.

Johnson's two sons work with him. He says it is possible to make $150 or more in a day doing this type of work. His secret is advertising by demonstration.

SPECIALIZED TREE AND SHRUBBERY TRIMMING

This is an excellent field either on a part-time or full-time basis. There is good money in it, and it doesn't necessarily require a lot of specialized training if you can learn by doing. My personal recommendation would be to get all the information you can about it through a good nursery before venturing out on an actual job.

The amount of equipment required depends largely on the individual. It is possible to start a business of this kind using a shrubbery saw fastened to a long pole. This kind of saw costs only a few dollars. Most tree and shrubbery trimmers today use a motor-driven chain saw which costs about $300. You might want to buy ladders, clippers and planting equipment if you wish to include shrubbery and tree installation in your service.

Allyne Kendall and Brad Williams are two young men who went into this business in Phoenix, Arizona, where there is a great deal of palm tree trimming work available. They make anywhere from $50 to $100 a day specializing in this particular tree.

PROFESSIONAL LANDSCAPE GARDENING

This is a field where the creative person can find unlimited possibilities. Landscape gardening requires a great deal of know-how, but if you have a green thumb, are eager to learn all you can about growing things, and have artistic talents, you should explore the possibilities of this profession.

Cal Crozier started out selling trees, plants, shrubs and disinfectants. As his home town grew he saw a need to provide a service for people who didn't know how to take care of their yards and grounds. He started small, doing little jobs, but in three years built a business that handles 70 percent of the landscaping in the area with almost more customers than it can handle.

He puts in landscape walks with waterfalls, fountains, arbors and railroad ties customers can use in their yards. People see these things, and then want the firm to do their landscaping.

INNOVATIONS SECRET TO SUCCESS

Crozier's is a very innovative firm. When I talked with Cal the last time he spoke of putting in a fish pond stocked with carp (Koi fish) which do very well in the local climate. He is doing all the work on the pond himself. Crozier expects big sales from this fish pond alone, because it is something, he says, that everyone will want. They can be made in any size or design.

The phenomenal success of this firm, in an area flooded with landscape artists, is obviously due to much ingenuity. Crozier is not offering just another landscape service, but one with something extra.

Crozier says a person can start in business on a small scale with about $1,000. He will need shovels, rakes, picks for hard rocks and trowels for trowler cement or mortar. If a man is creative, Crozier says, it is possible to net from $20,000 to $30,000 a year in this business.

TOOL OR IMPLEMENT RENTAL

There is definitely a tremendous demand for tool rental services because many people start in business without enough capital to purchase all the expensive equipment they need. The field is wide open as to what type of rentals a person wants to offer. There are few limitations: just about anything can be offered successfully for rent.

The one drawback to this business is the fact that in most cases it would take a sizeable sum of money to start, possibly $100,000 or more. This, however, isn't insurmountable: there are many ways to finance a business venture whether it be large or small. There is also a definite market for rentals on a smaller scale which would not require such a large investment. Some smaller pieces of equipment wouldn't be good rental items because they are easily obtainable. The secret is finding that spot someplace in between large and very small equipment items.

The small businessman who needs equipment but doesn't want to go into the really big items does need a means of securing temporary equipment when he starts out. If equipment rental business appeals to you, check into the items most generally rented and see if you can find that missing link. If you can, you will have for yourself a new-styled business.

Some of our biggest rental businesses today started on a shoestring. U-Haul, for example, began with a homemade hauling trailer.

On the other side of the fence, if you are going into a business that requires expensive equipment, take a look at rental possibilities for your own needs. A number of small businesses have found it more practical to rent equipment than to buy in the early stages of their operations. It might be a means of starting on much less capital. This is the way Allyne Kendall and Brad Williams were able to start their tree trimming business. They rented a saw until they had earned the necessary money to buy their own.

OPERATING A SPECIAL SERVICE FOR THE ELDERLY

Glen Reeves was a first-rate paper hanger who decided to concentrate his efforts in a senior citizen community. He knew these people had been bilked a lot of times because so many tradespeople have the misconception that residents of a special senior citizen community are wealthy. Reeves knew that many of these older people get by on very little money, and that a good craftsman, with their interests foremost in his mind, could develop a highly profitable and mutually beneficial business here.

Rather than saddle himself with the usual handicap of traveling great distances to handle the business, he bought a small trailer home and settled within close proximity to the senior citizen community.

His first objective was service to the customer as opposed to working the area for a quick, easy buck. In a senior citizen community most of the people know each other, so word gets around in a hurry. In Reeves' case this was a big advantage: he had only to do paper hanging for a few residents before the rest heard about his work. He soon had all the customers he could handle. The secret to his success was quality work for fair prices and total dependability.

HOW TO BREAK INTO THIS FIELD

Reeves offers this advice to anyone wishing to learn the craft. He says varied experience for a short time is better than many years working in one specialized area. He suggests serving an apprenticeship under someone who does all types of jobs.

The equipment needed to start includes a paste table, straight-edged trestles, two stepladders, dropcloths, hand tools, razor blade knives, screwdrivers, pliers, a small hammer and two six-inch broad knives. You will also need two smoothing brushes, measuring tape, single-edge razor blades, two small paint brushes and a roller.

Transportation for you and your equipment is a must. A used station wagon will serve the purpose well. You should be able to purchase one for about $500. The basic equipment costs will amount to approximately $200 in addition to this. This is something that can easily be started as a second-income occupation and developed into a full-time position with a potential income of $100 a day.

PERSONALIZED BEAUTY CARE IN CUSTOMER'S OR YOUR HOME

There are cosmetic representatives who give some forms of beauty treatment in the home but few full beauty services come to you. Some beauty shops do go to hospitals, nursing homes and other spots where a number of people who are confined need the service. How wonderful it would be to offer a service in the home to elderly people, shut-ins and others who are unable to travel to a beauty shop for one reason or another!

Frequently I have used the services of beauty operators who worked out of their homes. In my case the advantage was their convenient hours. The home service operators were more flexible, and I could go at a time suitable to my working schedule. Both of these operators had successful businesses.

A service in your home is especially advantageous when it is inconvenient for you to work away from home. If you do not live in an area zoned for business, you may have problems with licensing. There are some hairdressers who operate without advertising their service other than by word of mouth, but this may not be legal in some areas.

Clara R. just missed out on a college scholarship. When she didn't have enough money for school expenses she started doing students' hair in their rooms to earn extra money.

Beauticians in the area complained that she didn't have a license. When Clara told them she'd have to quit school to obtain one, the beauticians got together, helped her get that license and made it possible for her to work her way through college.

Her expenses were only the cost of a license and a few supplies. She earned approximately $600 over and above her college costs and living expenses. Where there's a will there's a way!

9

Secrets of Big Money in Product Manufacturing

Service-type businesses are sometimes started with less capital investment than those involving a tangible product because many services require very little, if any, merchandise in stock.

A tangible item, however, is often the easiest to market. A good product with eye appeal, one that fills a need or desire, frequently sells itself. Millions of dollars are spent every year on products; many fortunes have been built from the creation and development of one small item. If you enjoy working with your hands and like to create new and interesting objects, product manufacturing may be your forte.

You don't have to be a genius to become a success in this field. You need only a little imagination and a willingness to try. These are the most common traits among successful product manufacturers.

You may find something with unique appeal just by making gifts for your friends or family or you may, like Dan Gerber of Gerber Products Co., uncover an unfilled need. Gerber started producing canned baby foods when he discovered, from personal experience, how difficult and messy it was to puree baby foods at home.

Your product discovery may be even simpler than this. Maybe something you are making right now in your home has a marketing potential which you never realized.

A MANUFACTURING BUSINESS IN YOUR HOME

You don't need a huge manufacturing or production plant such as Gerber had to start a product manufacturing business of your own. Some of the most successful businesses today started in a room or garage of a house. A good example is the Honda Company, which started as a home business and is today the largest motorcycle producer in the world.

The important thing is not so much what you have to start with—whether you make a small beginning or can start big. What really matters is whether you have the courage to begin.

The person who must make a simple beginning at home has some advantages over the person with more capital. Too frequently, the person with big capital delves in too deeply before really knowing the business, and then loses everything. The sheer necessity to begin slowly, with little capital, can easily make the difference between failure and success.

Since you are interested particularly in a second income operation, you may find it more satisfactory to start at home. The time convenience is often the most valuable asset of an "after hours" business; no extra traveling time is necessary. A manufacturing business in your home then can serve a twofold purpose. It gives you a convenient and time-saving operating base for moonlighting in your off hours, and also an economical way to start a small business which can easily grow into a larger one.

CHOOSING YOUR PRODUCT

Many factors go into selecting a suitable product for manufacture. Probably a large percentage of items are produced in the beginning because someone enjoys making them, and are later discovered, quite by accident, to be salable. It is far better, however, to eliminate the element of chance wherever possible in order to assure the greatest possible opportunity for success.

First, take a good look at your assets and special abilities. Make a list of every possible item you feel you might enjoy making and any products you already know how to create.

Choose the type of market you would most like to reach. Do you want to sell directly to individuals or would you prefer to sell wholesale to stores or other retail businesses?

If you want to start with individuals, then try some of the items on your friends either verbally or with actual sample items. See what seems to have the most appeal.

For a greater sale range on a smaller margin of profit, retail outlets should be investigated. In some cases it might be necessary to produce some items to place on consignment in a few stores. The store doesn't have to gamble anything on the product under this arrangement; you receive pay only when your products are sold. It also gives you a chance to see what sells and what doesn't before you are in too deep.

This method of selecting a product allows you an opportunity to find something you enjoy making which also appeals to the general public. But there is nothing that can beat the production of an item or items for which you already know there is a need or a desire, such as Gerber's realization that there was a need for canned baby food.

The product doesn't have to fill a practical need such as this. It may, instead, be something with strong personal appeal or that is a popular item of the times. Jewelry is a perfect example of this.

The selection might be something that appeals to the funny bone. A housewife living close to a school bought various items and turned them into joke pieces. One of her products was a can on which she painted the words, "Fresh Air." She set aside a room in her house to display these items and invited the students from the nearby school to come take a look. She started selling immediately and has grossed as much as $1,000 in a day. The investment for this would be minimal: many of the materials used can be discards.

So there are several different approaches to choosing the most salable product. Filling a specific need such as Gerber and Honda did is a reasonably certain formula for success, but a need to laugh, on which the housewife capitalized, or the desire for unusual luxury items can't be overlooked. The quality of your product and how you promote it have a lot to do with making your selection a success.

ONE INGREDIENT WHICH GUARANTEES BIG RETURNS

There is one ingredient absolutely essential to a successful product manufacturing venture with substantial financial returns. It is a good marketing technique.

That the ability to properly market your product is more important than the product itself is evidenced by the success of several nationally known products on the market today. Some of these give proof that even an inferior product can become successful if properly marketed. The combination of a good product with the right marketing plan should be unbeatable.

The best way for the novice to learn marketing techniques is to talk with the experts. Seek out the marketing professionals in or near your community. Talk to trade buyers, store managers, manufacturer representatives who sell the product and write the orders, and the manufacturing plant owners who have successfully marketed a product. Ask them questions and explain your specific needs. Then, with the help of their advice, evolve a plan for your product that will gain its wide acceptance.

Don't be hesitant about asking the experts. You'll find most of these people eager and willing to help someone who really wants to learn and do a job.

SELECTING THE BEST POSSIBLE OUTLETS

To assure the most favorable situation when you select the product you wish to manufacture and sell, it is necessary to study the outlets available to you for merchandising it.

A great deal of time can be wasted in placing your merchandise in second-rate outlets—places that don't have the type of trade suited to your particular merchandise. While it is true, as Emerson said, a superior product will sell in any location and under most circumstances, carefully selected outlets will certainly speed the process.

If you are interested in building a volume business which can grow into a full-time affluent income, you will probably prefer wholesale. While your margin of profit is considerably lower in wholesale merchandising than in retail, the volume is what makes the difference.

This doesn't mean you can't have a highly profitable retail business. If this is what you enjoy, go to it. You can make real profits with correct merchandising.

Your main consideration, whether you sell wholesale or retail, should be that the merchandise is placed in a location suitable to its particular characteristics. You wouldn't want to place delicate chinaware in a store for lawn care equipment. You need to find a store that has other porcelain or ceramic items, perhaps, or other types of merchandise allied with chinaware.

There is no real shortcut to finding these ideal outlets. It takes a lot of time and effort to select the right one. You will need to walk the streets and explore, firsthand, the kind of shops suitable for your product. When you find shops that carry similar merchandise, you will need to investigate several other factors: How well do they display their merchandise? What kind of clientele do they have? How large a volume of business are they doing? You can't just wander by and select any nice-looking store on first sight. You must do a study of the total operation each time you select an outlet. Once this is done, if you have a superior product to place in these properly selected outlets, you have all the ingredients of a financially success-ful business.

UNCOVERING THE SECRETS OF SUPPLY AND DEMAND

One of the most accurate ways to discover products that are in demand is to do a survey. This can be done by mail, by direct door-to-door contact or by meeting numerous groups.

The important factor in conducting a survey is using an approach which makes people want to cooperate with you. This can be accomplished by phrasing your questions in such a way the respondents will realize that their cooperation will benefit them personally. For example, ask them for descriptions or names of products they would like to purchase but haven't been able to locate. Get as much detailed information from them about these products as possible. This information will not only give you details on the product itself, but it will give you excellent material for future promotion if you do decide to manufacture it.

If you already have a specific product in mind, you can create the necessary demand for it with proper promotion. Big companies spend huge sums of money to instill a desire for their product in the minds of potential buyers long before the product is on the market. The small business person can't spend this kind of money to promote, but he can do it in a smaller way, starting on a gradient scale and gradually building the promotion into a larger operation.

You can develop a product—a piece of jewelry, a unique piece of craftwork or whatever—and wear it, display it in your home or, better still, in public places where large numbers of people will see it and admire it.

Items that need to be replenished or that people wish to replenish often are sure guarantees for constant resale. These can be either necessity or luxury items. Jewelry is a good example of the latter.

You can create the demand for almost anything you wish to supply, if you make a good enough product and let enough people know you have it for sale.

SPARE TIME JEWELRY MAKING ZOOMED TO HUGE PROFITS

Jim David, who puttered with hand tools since he was a child, started making silver and turquoise jewelry as a hobby, then suddenly found himself in a zooming full-time business. Actually it is as full-time as he wants to make it, depending on how much money he wants to earn.

He makes $500 or more in a 40-hour week without stress or strain. "Sometimes I work much longer hours for a couple of weeks," he says, "then take off for two weeks or so. I start again when I need to replenish my bank account."

His method of promoting his product is simple. He displays his jewelry wearing lots of it himself. This attracts attention to the items.

He sells strictly wholesale. The profit is less, but the volume of sales is greater and the bookkeeping is less involved.

This young jeweler thinks the most important thing in this business is having an affinity for the product. He wouldn't recommend it to anyone who doesn't have a strong liking for this kind of jewelry.

The business can be started at a cost of about $300. More equipment can be purchased as merchandise is sold. To start, you need a work bench that is compact but durable, a pounding surface or a short log standing on end, and an anvil. A heat source for an acetylene and air torch will be necessary; regular city gas and compressed air can be used. You will also need a four- or six-inch jeweler's saw with various blades, an alcohol lamp, a pair of 10- or 11-inch tin shears, a ring mandrel and a small bench vise. You can purchase a charcoal block from jewelry supply or silver supply houses. Hammers needed are a rawhide mallet, a half-inch machinist (ball peen) hammer. You will want two pairs of six- or seven-inch tweezers and an eight- or nine-inch pair, flat-nose and round-nose pliers, and side cutters. You will need an asbestos pad for protecting the table. It should be at least half an inch thick and 12 by 12 inches in size. Also required are a bezel pusher, a French burnisher, a fine half round jeweler's file and a handle.

David gained most of his early information from the book *Indian Silversmithing* by W. Ben Hunt, published by Bruce Publishing Company, Milwaukee, Wisconsin in 1952.

Turquoise is the popular stone for this type of jewelry in the western states, but it can be made with other stones. If silver jewelry appeals to you and you don't live in the Southwest, there are probably some stones characteristic to your part of the country that would make equally beautiful pieces of jewelry.

HOW TO PRODUCE SOMETHING DIFFERENT IN WAX

Candle making has been a popular pastime for a long time. It can be very profitable if you use a bit of ingenuity.

I discovered a drug rehabilitation group that made some remarkable seasonal items: an entire Christmas scene with trees, houses, candy canes and everything associated with Christmas. This could also be done for Easter, St. Patrick's Day, Independence Day, May Day and every special day throughout the year as well as special occasions such as weddings, birthdays and graduations.

This same group discovered a way to salvage the imperfect candles. They put one of these old mold candles in a tub of water, then pour wax heated to about 225 degrees around the old mold candle while turning it in the water. All kinds of fantastic shapes result—castles, trees, houses. There are many ways, also, to make imitation decoupage with candles.

To start a candle-making business some of the basic items you will need are two ten-gallon pots, preferably used; a thermometer; wax; scent; color; pouring and measuring devices; a sand pit and sand bags. These could be purchased for about $100. One group started with only $25 and purchased more material as they sold the candles. With careful planning and inexpensive equipment it is possible to make as much as $300 from a $100 investment.

LEATHER GOODS WITH SPECIAL APPEAL

Leather items are popular, especially when made with superb craftsmanship. Purses, wallets, sandals, jackets and belts are not unique items in themselves, but they can become outstandingly different if the leather artist adds that extra touch. Among the items that sell well when properly made are key rings, watch bands, berets, plant hangers, caps, moccasins, custom clothing, briefcases and coats.

Many items can be made from scraps. Multicolored purses, jackets, afghans, patchwork skirts and caps are just a few.

If working with leather appeals to you, start exploring leather shops and mail order catalogues, then decide what you can add to the market that is different.

LEATHER SHOP PROVIDES GOOD INCOME FOR YOUNG COUPLE

Gary and Marsha Minniss learned leathercraft from friends who operated a leather shop. They then started their own shop in a garage, calling it "The Leather Garage." They made only leather caps which they wholesaled to leather shops around the country. This enabled them to see and study a variety of leather businesses.

For a time the Minnisses rented retail space in someone else's shop while continuing their wholesale cap business. In four months they were ready to go into a building of their own. They took it one step at a time, learning everything they could about the business. Before opening their own shop, Gary and Marsha made a list of all the things successful leather shops had in common. Then they set out to find a location most suitable for putting that list to work.

In their chosen location they have now expanded their own successful business to cover many items, and are continually adding more. Both wholesale and retail businesses are doing well.

To start a wholesale leather cap business such as the one operated by Gary and Marsha Minniss, you would need an industrial sewing machine, leather scissors, a heavy-duty stapler and a supply of leather. The cost could be reduced somewhat if you purchase a used sewing machine.

For a shop you need several additional items—dyes, glue, a strap cutter, buckles, leather, bottom and top soles, makeup models, belt buckles and latches for purses. You would probably also want stamping tools, a mallet, a piece of marble, edging tools, a square and an awl. The cost for these items is around $2,000. Average earnings in this business would be about $600 a month, but it is possible to make as much as $2,000 a month.

UNDISCOVERED PROFITS FROM SCRAPS

There are so many ways to make money from scraps it would be easy to write a whole chapter on the subject.

The head of a large manufacturing plant in Texas made it all through scrap metal. He started his first wrecking yard from a total savings of $100. This formerly poverty-stricken boy is now a multimillionaire with plants in several cities.

Anyone with a small truck can start this business without big capital; there are numerous places to pick up scraps of metal. I know of one man who bids on the electric fixtures in torn-down houses. He sells these at a good profit.

Wallpaper scraps make attractive wastebaskets, lamps, vases, gift wrappings and many other items. The possibilities are limited only be your imagination. Your capital outlay will be small: most paper hangers will be happy to save scraps for you, and you can purchase lamps and other items inexpensively, even picking up used merchandise at little cost. What makes such items sell for a good price is the effective way you make use of the wallpaper scraps.

Kenneth and Elizabeth King collect driftwood and carve birds from these bits and pieces of scrap wood which they find on shores and along dry washes of rivers and streams. They do their work entirely by hand using no coloring except oil stains. They use nothing but driftwood both for the bird and for the base on which it stands.

A boat is helpful in their wood collecting but it is not essential. An adequate boat costs from $300 to $1,000. They also use a hand saw and a big chopping knife. The Kings make their own carving knives from old straight razors. The best places to look for these are in antique shops and secondhand stores. They also use lots of sandpaper and an oil base for the final finish. The cost is about $100 for these items, and their average income is around $500 a month.

A real estate man, when he gets a listing for a house, takes discarded furniture and other scrap items and turns them into profit with garage sales.

An energetic housewife cleans garages in exchange for any "throw-away" items. She sells these in a "bargain barn," and is doing a $50,000 annual business. Your stock in this business costs nothing, and you can wait until it is paying well before you need to rent or own a building. Until then you can work out of your home.

TAKING YOUR LOCK AND KEY SERVICE TO THE CUSTOMER

Bill Summers, a retired Air Force man, started his portable lock and key service in the trunk of his car with an investment of approximately $1,500. Two and a half years later he had a fully equipped camper on a truck and a business worth $25,000 in equipment. He uses an answering serice to be on call 24 hours a day. It's possible to clear $60 a day in this business after overhead.

Basic equipment needed to start on a small scale would include a small key machine, a tool box, a set with springs for re-pinning locks, special tools and a stock of current key blanks.

Summers advises anyone starting this business to study and learn the craft well. He took his training through a correspondence school, working at the trade as he learned. His motto today is "a satisfied customer always," and his repeat business is proof of the workability of such a philosophy.

PRODUCING SOMETHING DIFFERENT WITH FLOWERS

William A. Beale, a horticulturist, enjoys making artificial flower arrangements as a hobby. He picks up bits of manzanita wood in his state and turns them into natural-looking miniature bonsai trees.

The only stock required is a supply of shallow bowls with trays inside, mixing plaster, artificial flowers and leaves, glue and pebbles gathered from various spots. The cost is from $5 to $30 each; the finished products sell for $15 to $50 each.

Joan Smith, under the trade name of Flores Secas, "grows jewelry" in her own back yard using such flowers as verbenas, alyssums, onions and desert holly. She lets these go to seed and then picks their blossoms. She keeps these in a preserving material a few days, then, using jewelry mounts and flocked ribbon, makes them into pins, pendants and rings.

Supplies necessary to start this business could be purchased for less than $100 with additional purchases made as the merchandise is sold. Necessary items include jewelry findings of various sizes. A large pendant costs about $1.25; findings for rings cost from 55¢ to 75¢ each. You will need a ten-pound bag of sand, graded chalk in various colors, tweezers with a fine point and a high-intensity lamp. This close work may require a magnifying glass. Plastic sectioned boxes are suggested for storing different colored flowers. Joan uses three kinds of glue—epoxy for gluing the metal together, clear glue for gluing the flowers to the findings, and white glue for gluing the flocked backing into the jewelry. With proper promotion you should be able to make $200 a week at this craft.

"LOCAL COLOR" PRODUCTS FOR VISITORS OR TOURISTS

Every state in the United States has something distinctive to promote. This can become a thriving business for any enterprising craftsman. The opportunities here are not limited to tourists who visit the area: they can be promoted as gift items to be mailed elsewhere and sold all over the country through mail order advertising. Vermont maple syrup is a good example of a local tourist product which sells throughout the U.S. Walnuts and products made with walnuts have become popular items for mail order, as has Wisconsin cheese.

A couple in Massachusetts started selling jams and jellies made from special fruits growing in that part of the country. This small beginning soon developed into a full-time operation with a quaint little shop that sells a wide variety of items particularly characteristic of that area.

I myself sold a hand-painted western stationery line wholesale to shops all over our state. The stationery and bridge items had the appearance of expensive hand-painted work. They were handpainted, but we used an assembly line approach. We printed the basic designs in large quantities, then filled in the bits of color. We knew exactly where each color went, so the operation was automatic and large quantities could be painted in short periods of time.

The materials required for this project included paper for the stationery and bridge items, a set of paints, fine paint brushes and cellophane paper. It required less than $500 to make 100 percent profit on each packaged item.

A very simple tourist item was designed by a man in the eastern part of the country using old railroad spikes. He collected the spikes, painted the name of a town on them and sold them in quantity to tourists.

PREPARING ANTIQUES FOR SALE

You can develop a highly profitable business if you know antiques and are able to restore them to their natural state without too much time and effort.

Machines have been developed which remove the paints and varnishes from furniture surfaces in a matter of minutes using no water or heat. Most people don't know how to do a good job of stripping furniture; too often they use sandpaper which eliminates some of the top surface beauty. If you are interested in developing an antique business, you might want to investigate the possibility of utilizing a process such as this.

Antiques are a good business offering exceptional profits for those who know their product. There are many methods of merchandising. The consolidated flea markets for collectors of antiques seem to have gained considerable popularity over the years. Antique fairs offer another opportunity for quantity sales.

AMATEUR POTTER BECOMES WELL PAID POTTERY ARTIST

Muriel Flood was a former political scientist involved in diplomatic services who became a volunteer in a social service activity. She suddenly found herself facing a situation which could easily wipe out all her independent income. Her interests had been mostly intellectual over the years. She had done little with her hands, but she did study ceramics at one time and decided to update her information in this field. In a short period of time she developed a special knack for this craft and began working at it in earnest.

Now she has a full-time business producing a superior handmade ceramic line known as Fire and Earth Stoneware.

"Pottery is a competitive field," she said, "but each piece I make is an original, and I make sure the quality is of the best."

She has built her volume of business through craft fairs, art galleries, word-of-mouth advertising and several good newspaper articles She makes an additional income from teaching the craft to others.

Necessary equipment and stock are a kiln with shelves and stilts, a wheel, clay and glazes. These are the basic needs for a modest beginning and will run about $1,500. Within about a two-year period you can be making around $1,000 a month.

Muriel suggests getting into at least one good gallery as soon as you can. This is one of the best ways to promote and become known.

MANY WAYS TO PROMOTE

Whatever business you go into, you will need to do a satisfactory promotion job in order to insure top success.

In some cases people become known among friends and acquaintances before they actually start a business; this may be the factor that made them decide to turn a talent into profit. Such people are not totally unknown in their field, but they are not well known enough to make their business big and prosperous. It is necessary for every business person to publicize themselves and their product to the general public as quickly and as widely as possible.

Many ways of doing this have been discussed; each individual must choose the method which best suits his particular situation.

If you have a sizeable amount of money available for advertising, a big advertising campaign is probably the best assurance of success as long as the product promised is delivered. Most of us don't have that kind of money, however. Fortunately there are many less expensive routes you can follow.

Small classified ads in the newspaper offer an effective advertising medium at a small cost. Fliers with special coupons for free or discounted merchandise distributed in your area can bring in a good amount of business in the beginning.

There are free neighborhood newspapers in most communities that reach several thousand people. Their ad rates are low, and they can be effective. Radio spots are usually not too expensive a way to get your message to a sizeable number of prospective customers.

If there are fairs where you can display your merchandise, take advantage of these. You may also want to place your merchandise in stores, banks or other public places. You might need to make an arrangement to pay a small percentage to the store when any merchandise is sold through such a display.

Look around you and see what type of promotion is working for others. If it applies to your situation, use it.

DISTINGUISHING BETWEEN THE SALABLE AND THE UNSALABLE

While it is true that you can sell most any item if you make it superior to any other similar product on the market, it is better to start with a piece of merchandise which has considerable sale potential.

Some of the tests it should pass are:

Does it fill a known need? Is it something that is wanted? Is it better than any other such item now on the market? Can it be promoted easily?

If these few basic questions can be answered affirmatively, you have a salable product and are ready for business.

10

New and Unusual Ways to Make Money from Writing

This chapter is written particularly for the nonprofessional—the person who may never have tried to earn a living from writing. It is not written for the skilled author who writes and sells magazine articles and stories and is well versed in professional writing techniques.

There are many ways you can earn good money writing even though you have never attempted it before.

Numerous writing markets require no "literary talent." Some of these pay very well, offering an ideal sideline with flexible hours and many rewards.

If writing is something you have always wanted to do, here are some of the secrets that can open the door for you to this fascinating and profitable field. There are, also, a number of allied fields that provide excellent opportunities for part-time or full-time businesses.

MAKING SHORT PARAGRAPHS PAY OFF

Many magazine editors use short paragraphs throughout their publications to close up holes left by articles or stories that did not quite fill the space. A short paragraph or filler might be a child's cute saying, a joke, a human interest story, light verse, an information item or any number of short pieces, usually of 50 words or less. Writing style is not important here. It is the information that counts.

A quick glance through any of the slick magazines will give you a good idea of the structure of a filler. Different magazines run different types of fillers—based on the particular reader interest of that publication.

This is an excellent field for the beginning writer; you don't need to be established to sell fillers to a large number of magazines. The secret of making good money in this area is volume production—turning out a great deal of material regularly. Some of the most successful filler writers keep as many as 50 small items in the mail all the time.

FINDING YOUR MARKETS

The actual pay per word is generally good in this market. It is extremely high, in fact, in some publications—often $1 a word or more. *Reader's Digest* is one of the best markets for filler material: it has several specialized categories for these short pieces as well as space at the bottom of its pages for general fillers. The magazine pays anywhere from $10 to $200 for small fillers.

Other good markets include *Playboy, New Yorker, Good Housekeeping* and *Mechanics Illustrated.* These are only a small portion of the market. There are all kinds of opportunities for filler material on a wide variety of subjects.

The most complete reference source for this field that I know of is the book, *Writing and Selling Fillers and Short Humor,* edited by A.S. Burach and containing contributions from a number of writers. It is published by The Writer, Inc.

WRITING ADVERTISING COPY AND MARKETING IT

Good copywriters can usually find work, because every business needs some form of advertising and many small operations cannot afford full-time advertising people. Some advertising agencies, too, prefer to use freelance copywriters and artists instead of regular staff members in this type of position.

Whether you are experienced or not, there are many opportunities in this field through advertising agencies and individual business firms where such sevice is needed. It pays anywhere from $10 to $30 an hour.

For the creative individual who isn't an experienced copywriter but who is interested in learning the field, it isn't too difficult to acquire the skill. Study other people's copy. Choose a particular field of business for which you would like to write advertising copy, then study every ad you can find on that subject. Go to your local library and make copies of all the old ads a particular firm has used over a period of time. Work on those ads until you have made definite improvements. Take your version to the business manager and show him where your ad is certain to bring in more business. Ask for an opportunity to do his ads.

If you can handle other related jobs along with writing advertising copy there are many exciting opportunities available to you which don't require professional skill or training.

COPYWRITER GETS POSITION WITH SHOPPING CENTER

June L. was a self-taught advertising copywriter in a large eastern city when her husband's work made it necessary for them to move to a small town. She had doubts about being able to get a good advertising job in the new location and had almost resigned herself to being a full-time housewife, giving up her sideline. Her plans were changed soon after they arrived when she found a job which enabled her to utilize her past experience in writing advertising copy and to develop new creative skills as well. She became the advertising director for a shopping center. In this new position she wrote ad copy and handled all promotions for the mall. She even learned to write news releases about activities in the mall.

June operated out of her home, working flexible hours. She makes from $150 to $200 a week.

In some shopping centers the advertising director operates out of an office on location, but in the small malls this is usually not a full-time occupation. A part-time job in a small mall can easily lead to a full-time position in a larger shopping center, where the potential is unlimited.

The secret to a successful career in this field lies in researching all you can about other shopping center operations. June recommends that anyone interested in this kind of work subscribe to the *Shopping Center Newsletter.* It is published monthly by the National Research Bureau in Burlington, Iowa and contains detailed information and ideas for handling all types of mall promotions.

STARTING SMALL AND GROWING BIG

Many would-be writers become discouraged early in the game because they haven't observed the old adage that it is better to crawl before you walk. It is wise to get experience in some lower-paying areas before you try the big markets. Often potential writers try the big markets immediately, then give up after one or two rejections. For this reason I feel it is better, as a general rule, to start on a small scale with something simple and fairly easy to market.

In my case, I started a writing career with no professional training of any kind. The only study I did was of the magazines themselves. I was interested in writing for juvenile magazines because it seemed like an easier market to master. All I did was read a number of these publications, mostly small religious papers. Then I started writing and sending my material—fiction and non-fiction—to magazines geared to children and teenagers. I didn't make much money, only ½¢ to 1¢ a word, but I learned a lot about writing. It was excellent experience and training because juvenile writing must be done in simple language, and almost any writing is better when worded simply. That background has stood me in good stead over the years. Simplicity in writing is the secret to success in many fields of writing.

EDITORS EXCELLENT TEACHERS

One of the biggest advantages I found in writing for these small juvenile magazines was the constructive criticism I received from the editors. It was better than going to school or taking a special course in writing.

They would often write detailed criticisms on my stories and articles. At the same time they also offered encouragement. It was that encouragement that made me persevere. This is the real secret to success in this field—continuing to write—never giving up.

HOW TO COMPETE WITH THE PROFESSIONAL

The secret of being a professional writer is acting as if you are a professional at all times. Don't ever put yourself down or indicate in any way that you are not a professional. Nobody will know what you have or don't have unless you tell them. Study books on motivation and develop the ability to sell yourself and your abilities. Read such authors as Elmer Wheeler, Merlyn Cundiff, James Allen, L. Ron Hubbard and Orison Swett. Make every day count, and always feel, act and speak like a professional, knowing you are one. Never let anything discourage you.

WINNING THROUGH PERSISTENCE

Bev Barney sent out 100 examples of her food column to state newspapers. She waited what seemed an endless time with no response. She got only one reply from a weekly newspaper, one she thought would be of small value to her. Writing for this paper turned out to be one of the most productive stepping stones in her career.

LEARNING FROM CRITICISM

Be willing at all times to accept constructive criticism: it can be the very thing that turns defeat into success.

Once when I worked on a project that required an entirely different type of writing from my usual style, I put together what I thought was a great piece of work which all my friends praised highly. I sent it to the man for whom I was doing the work, and he returned it with harsh criticism. My friends were insulted and defensive in my behalf, but I decided to follow the suggestions and see if I could improve upon the piece. When I did, my critic was totally satisfied, and I had learned a whole new style of writing.

Later I did another writing assignment for the same man, and he accepted this piece without changing one word. I had learned my lesson. It has paid off ever since.

DEVELOPING PROFESSIONAL SKILLS WITHOUT LEAVING HOME

Writing is one profession that can be learned at home as easily as in school because there is a great deal of valid instruction material available. Most of it can be assimilated very satisfactorily on an individual basis, and writing is definitely a profession where much of the learning is accomplished through doing. Many a successful author has proved the validity of the old saying that "practice makes perfect."

HOW TO FIND HELPFUL WRITING AIDS

There is a considerable amount of published material on writing techniques. Check your local library for books on the subject and subscribe to writers' magazines. Most of them carry helpful articles by successful authors. You can purchase a small tape recorder for about $20 and listen to a wide variety of lessons and lectures on writing methods. These will aid your professional development considerably. There are a number of good correspondence courses on this subject too, covering both fiction and non-fiction. These offer the advantage of individualized criticism. Most correspondence schools are advertised in one or more of the writers' magazines.

Bev Barney's secret of successful writing is putting whatever she writes on tape, and then listening to see how well it reads. She finds this an excellent way to smooth out the rough spots.

Once you have studied the material the most important action is putting it into practice. You will learn as much by doing as you do by studying, so have at it—there is no other way. The most successful writers got where they are today by writing several hundred words every day. You can do it too. There is no better teacher than experience itself, so start writing. Write, write, write!

HIDDEN OPPORTUNITIES FOR THE NON-PROFESSIONAL

There are many ways to become a published writer and thereby move into the professional bracket. One of the quickest methods is by writing a regular column for one or more small-town newspapers.

To locate all these periodicals in your state, check with the metropolitan newspaper nearest you and ask to buy a current statewide newspaper directory. It shouldn't cost much more than $5 to get a list of all the weeklies and dailies published in your state. Once you have this directory you can write to editors and publishers, sending them samples of your column. You might also want to give them suggestions for other subject matter on which you feel qualified to write.

The secret to establishing your name as a writer is to write under your own byline in as many publications as possible, even if your initial pay is small. Writing a regular column for small newspapers is an excellent means of developing the necessary discipline required of any successful pro.

Bev Barney started by writing for one weekly. Now she writes for a whole chain of weeklies with a total circulation of well over a quarter million.

WRITING ABOUT A FAMILIAR SUBJECT

Bev's success in selling her column to a number of papers resulted from writing about a subject on which she was well informed—cooking and special recipes.

"I'm not a good writer," she says. "I'm just a good cook."

To aid you in developing material write to *PR Aids' Periodicals, Inc.,* 221 Park Avenue South, New York, New York. 10003, asking to be put on the mailing list for their newsletter. It will cut down on your research activity and give you excellent material for columns.

SECRETS TO BECOMING A SUCCESSFUL JOURNALIST

Many successful journalists started somewhere at the bottom and worked up, learning all they could about the business as they went. They saw a chance to get a foot in the door and took it. To do this you must be on the lookout for every opportunity—no matter how small—and be ready to grab it.

Sometimes the best place to start is with a weekly paper. These small periodicals frequently need part-time writers. In such a position you can gain valuable experience while still holding down another job.

Internships available to journalism students during the summer often lead to permanent positions later. The teen sections of newspapers sometimes hire students to write for the paper while they are still in school. Many of these young journalists have secured full-time jobs with that same paper when they completed their schooling. Today's journalism students have quite a few doors opened to them, but the secret to success for many a journalist has been the willingness to seek out a door, then open it.

CLASSIFIED AD CLERK BECOMES WOMEN'S PAGE EDITOR

Jeanne Tro Williams had no training or college degree, but she had a goal and the necessary determination to attain it. This was the secret to her success. She had done a little writing off and on since she was a teenager, but what she really wanted to do was write for a large metropolitan newspaper. To accomplish this she was willing to do whatever was necessary.

She took a job as a classified ad clerk and proved her abilities so well that she soon became a classified supervisor. While working in this position she kept her eyes open for possible opportunities to demonstrate her writing ability. She finally persuaded the public relations department to give her an opportunity in that section. Here Jeanne was hired on a trial basis for one month only, but she stayed five years. By that time her superiors became more and more aware of her ability. She finally landed a job in the Women's Forum section of a large daily paper. Six years later she became the Women's Forum editor.

LOCAL CORRESPONDENT FOR TRADE PUBLICATIONS

One of the most commonly overlooked yet most productive markets for writers is in business and trade journals. These are monthly publications which buy more material from freelance writers than all the other markets combined.

Many people have the misconception that it is necessary to have technical knowledge about specific subjects if you write for trade publications. This is a fallacy: the people who write for these publications are seldom experts in the field. The experts are too busy doing other things to write magazine articles, but not too busy to give this information to trade magazine writers.

GOOD RESEARCHER WRITES SUCCESSFULLY ABOUT TRADES

George H. knows nothing about mechanics. If something goes wrong with his car, he lifts the hood, looks underneath, shakes his head and says, "I don't know what's the matter with that thing." then he calls a good mechanic to take care of it for him. However, George H. sells articles regularly to such publications as *Autombile Rebuilder* and *Popular Mechanics.* He knows the type of information necessary for a good article, and asks experts for that information. After interviewing someone qualified to supply the necessary data, he puts this information into good writing form. The secret to success in this field is the ability to research technical information and report it accurately. This is more important than professional writing skill.

You can discover practically every trade journal published by looking through the appropriate section of the current *Writers Market.* This should be available in the reference section of your local library. Look around your community for unique promotions and innovative methods of operation by different businesses. When you find something you feel is salable, query the trade magazine serving that particular industry.

Many business and trade journal writers have reported earning as high as $25,000 a year.

PREPARING RESUMÉS AND COVER LETTERS

Frequently qualified people don't get jobs they apply for because they are inept at writing good resumés and cover letters. A good resumé and cover letter writer, properly promoted, can make a fortune, especially after a few of his clients experience success through his efforts. If this area of writing appeals to you, go to your local library and get all the books available on this type of writing and study them thoroughly.

Go to the personnel offices of a variety of businesses and discover what these people want to see on a resumé. Keep a file of sample resumés for as many different types of businesses as you can; then promote your service any way you can—through employment services, classified ads, and through satisfied customers. To get these, you may need to serve one or two free or at greatly reduced prices. Once the word gets around that your resumés do the job, you will have all the customers you can handle, and you can earn from $10 to $15 an hour in this field.

A FORTUNE MADE FROM ONE SALES LETTER

Writing sales letters requires a highly specialized technique. Very few business men and women know how to write letters that inspire others to buy their product, sight unseen, through the mails. This usually means they must hire an expert to write for them, paying top money for this service which brings in greater sales.

Thomas L. Hall wrote a sales letter for a manufacturer in Connecticut to promote the sale of this industry's product throughout the United States and Canada. His letter brought the company over $6,000,000 gross in sales over a two-year period. Hall was paid almost half a million dollars for the letter!

SPEECH WRITING AND HOW TO GET ASSIGNMENTS

The secret of developing a clientele and building a reputation as a speech writer is starting at an opportune time. One of the best times is during a political campaign. There are always politicians running for office who need help in this area. You wouldn't be able to write for any who were in competition with each other, but you can easily write speeches for several contenders on the same side of the fence who are not running for the same job.

Once you prove yourself an effective speech writer you will have no trouble finding steady clients among business executives, club officers and public-minded people. It is possible to make from $10 to $30 an hour in this field.

INCREASE YOUR INCOME FIVE TIMES WRITING FOR CHILDREN

Several years ago it was almost impossible to make a living wage writing in religious publications for children because the word rates were low. Today many of these particular juvenile magazines still pay only ½¢ to 2¢ a word, but a number of them which have special denominational readership—those that don't overlap each other—a few years ago started to allow multiple submissions. This means it is sometimes possible to submit the same story or article to as many as five small religious publications and, if you sell to all five, you increase your pay rate five times.

JUVENILE WRITER DISCOVERED SECRET

John R. had been writing for juvenile publications for a number of years, but the low pay made it impossible for him to make more than a meager supplemental income this way. He then discovered the secret to bigger money from small periodicals—multiple submissions. He queried these magazines and got written permission to sell the same material to as many as five different ones at a time. He didn't get wealthy from his writing efforts even then, but by increasing his income five times on most of the material he submitted, he earned from $6,000 to $8,000 a year.

MOVING INTO MORE PRODUCTIVE MARKETS

This was a stepping stone for John, as it has been for many of us. It enabled him to concentrate all his efforts on writing and gradually spread out into more lucrative areas.

He said there were many benefits in juvenile writing beyond the actual remuneration. He found the constructive criticism from those magazine editors far more beneficial than some of the paid courses he had taken.

Changes take place constantly in editorial policy, as in other areas, so it would be well to check each magazine separately before doing any multiple submissions to make sure this policy is still in effect. It would be necessary to get permission to do this from each publication anyway.

There are a number of children's publications in the religious field and outside it that pay good rates. As in any field of writing, the higher the pay scale the more difficult the sale, but there are many good markets for those who specialize in writing for children.

WRITING JUVENILE BOOKS

One of the most rewarding areas for the juvenile writer is in book manuscripts. The initial pay for children's books is not high, but the continuing sales, over a fairly long period of time, bring the income up considerably.

Clarice H. authored several children's books which were bought by one of the larger publishing houses. Her accumulated royalties brought her a sideline income of from $2,000 to $3,000 a year.

HOW TO UNCOVER NUMEROUS ALLIED FIELDS

There are a number of areas that tie in closely to the writing profession: you can discover most of these by studying writers' magazines. There are articles on a wide variety of related activities such as commercial art and photography. The advertisements in these magazines will also give you information about these other fields. Study them and select the area that best suits your talents. It could be a means of supporting your writing aspirations until they become adequately self-sustaining.

COMMERCIAL WORK FINANCED ARTIST INTO FAME AND MONEY

Roy Kerswill worked as a commercial artist six years for the Martin Company, makers of the Titan missile. Littly by little, as he worked there, he began painting western history and landscapes after his eight-hour day. One of the secrets to his outstanding success was his willingness to give up all his side interests and devote all his free after-work hours to painting.

He held his first art show in a rented downtown shop. When his painting sales increased, he quit the job and began devoting all his time to painting. Kerswill and his wife later bought some property in a mountain area and built a small gallery. Here he placed a group of his paintings along with the works of fifteen or sixteen other artists. This new business was a success almost immediately.

Today he paints exclusively and is no longer in the gallery business. Other galleries now handle his work. His paintings, which are included in many art collections throughout the country, bring premium prices.

EDITING MANUSCRIPTS

If you have a background in English composition, there are many writers who could use your help in editing their manuscripts for grammar and punctuation. They pay anywhere from $5 to $100 or more per job.

A small ad in any writers' magazine will get the word to writers. You should also contact your local press club. College students frequently need someone to edit their papers, and businessmen often need their speeches and other writings edited. The field is wide open. All you need to do is go after the business.

OFFERING A CLIPPING SERVICE TO WRITERS

Most writers are on the lookout for written material for a variety of writing projects and would welcome a source of clippings from magazines and newspapers.

You should file clippings according to subject matter and advertise them on a wide range of subjects. You might even want to include a customized clipping service where you agree to watch for and clip all items pertaining to a specific subject for individual clients.

To do this you will need to secure a directory of the newspapers in your state and subscribe to the most important ones. You can also get the Gebbie House Magazine Directory, P.O. Box 1111, Sioux City, Iowa, for about $40. This is a public relations and freelance guide to the nation's leading house magazines.

Advertise your clipping service for a $5 joining fee, $15 monthly charge and 15¢ for each article clipped.

DESIGNING BROCHURES, FLIERS, PROGRAMS

Many small businesses can use this service as an inexpensive way to advertise their products or services. If your talents are in the field of layout and artwork, this should be a reasonably easy and profitable venture for you.

Collect brochures, fliers and programs from businesses and organizations wherever you can find them. Develop some of these ideas into personalized promotion material for your prospective clients.

To establish yourself in this business, it might be well to design a brochure for a friend or two so you have examples to show to possible customers.

THE SECRETS TO MAKING BIG MONEY WITH YOUR CAMERA

Jay S. was working at a salaried job while doing photography and darkroom work on the side. When he realized his job was limiting the amount of money he could make with his camera, he resigned and started freelancing full time. He became a news hound, an ardent society page reader, a student of advertising copy, an observing traveler and an on-the-job photographer at a minute's notice. Jay also set up his own darkroom which enabled him to deliver the finished photograph quickly while the subject was still newsworthy.

He was able, without working long hours, to make at least $1,000 a month after expenses. His secret was constant alertness to picture opportunities and the ability to develop them promptly.

You can start a business such as this with good used equipment for as little as $300. New equipment would require an investment of from $1,000 to $2,000.

You will need a camera, preferably one which uses size 120

film; an enlarger; electric drum drier; electric washer; developing tanks and chemicals. You could, if necessary, get by without an electric drum drier but this would slow you down considerably. It is possible to use blotter rolls, but Jay doesn't advise this unless it is done with the thought of changing to the electric equipment in a short time.

SEVEN WAYS TO TURN YOUR CAMERA INTO CASH

1. Be on the watch for newsworthy pictures all the time. Jay saw a nine-car wreck on the highway. He took a lot of pictures and sold them to several newspapers.

2. Take wedding photos and develop a follow-up business from all the bridesmaids and attendants participating at each wedding.

3. Shoot pictures of buildings under construction and make arrangements with contractors to buy progress shots from you as the buildings go up.

4. Watch the papers for birth notices and photograph new babies.

5. Go to school proms and other dress-up affairs, taking pictures of individuals and groups.

6. Contact trade journalists and other writers to arrange to supply pictures for their magazine articles.

7. Contact advertising agencies in your area. They offer a wide variety of opportunities for camera work.

PRODUCING SLIDE PRESENTATIONS

Slide presentations offer many opportunities for a good photographer. If you also have the ability to write the script you have an ideal situation. You can also work with a writer; sometimes you may need only to take pictures that will fit an already written script. Schools, clubs and businesses are all prospective customers for slides to sell their programs, product or service.

RECEPTIONIST BECOMES PROFESSIONAL RETOUCHER

Bonnie Rockwell took a job as receptionist in a photography studio. There wasn't enough work to keep her busy, so she spent a lot of time exploring the business, asking questions and watching others work. Eventually she learned all details of the operation and started doing many tasks around the studio Soon she discovered she had a particular aptitude for photo retouching and began developing that skill more thoroughly

When the studio she was working for went out of business, she explored opportunities with other studios and discovered that there is always a demand for good retouchers. She began to freelance and now has accounts all over the country. The secret to her success is first-rate work and prompt delivery.

Bonnie has developed her business so she can work the year round, but her busy season is from July 15 through March 15. Her peak business comes at Christmas. High school senior pictures start in July and last through March 15.

Working approximately eight months a year, it is possible to make from $10,000 to $15,000 annually. You can start this type of business with an investment of around $400. You will need a retouching machine, magnifying glass, lead holders, graphite leads of different grades, red pencils, dyes, brushes and miscellaneous items as well as portrait negatives on which to work.

Bonnie is pretty much self taught, but she recommends lessons. Many professional retouchers teach their skill during the slow season. There are also courses offered by photography schools. It is often possible to get a job as an apprentice and learn while you earn.

A beginner can acquire a clientele by writing letters, telephoning, going personally to portrait studios and photo laboratories and advertising in trade magazines.

Bonnie says one of the many advantages of this profession is that she never has to leave her house except to go to the post office. This eliminates the need for the usual work wardrobe and cuts down transportation costs. You can also live wherever you please—in any part of the country.

OPPORTUNITIES ALL AROUND YOU

For the writer, the artist, the photographer there are opportunities everywhere. It's just a matter of seeking them out.

If the situation you are looking for is not immediately accessible to you, take the next best thing and keep working toward your real goal. You'll make it if you keep working at it.

11

Tips on Unusual Profit-Making Opportunities in Teaching

Teaching is a field offering unlimited opportunities to earn second-income money. There are as many subjects waiting to be taught as there are activities and skills. People are eager to develop know-how in every field of knowledge you have to offer.

If you are a good cook, carpenter, linguist, housekeeper, landscape artist, bricklayer, bookkeeper, seamstress, tailor—anything—there are others who would like to know what you know. Whatever work you pursue or business venture you undertake, teaching can provide you with an additional income and require very few added work hours.

Read this chapter carefully. It is for everyone—not just the professional teacher. You will discover through the experiences of many people a number of ways to extend your own skills to the benefit of others as well as yourself.

Teaching can be a very remunerative field. Its twofold purpose often results in greater income potential for you and for those you teach.

SECRETS OF DISCOVERING OPPORTUNITIES FOR THE NON-ACCREDITED

What is your background? What experience do you have that others might profit from knowing? The first thing you must do if you are interested in teaching as a second career is review your assets and discover what you have to offer others.

Gail P., who had been a PBX switchboard operator earlier in her life, found a part-time job in the inner city teaching the less advantaged how to become PBX operators. It was a rewarding experience for her. She didn't make big money, but the satisfaction of helping others learn to help themselves was her best pay. Rehabilitation centers of all kinds need people who can teach some kind of skill. You often don't need a teacher's certificate for this kind of teaching. All you need is the ability to tell others how to do a particular thing.

Even though you may not have experience in the fields where the needs are the greatest, if you are a good student, you can learn the skill and teach it.

Parks and Recreation Departments in practically every city, county and state are looking for teachers both for part-time and full-time work. Senior citizen centers offer another excellent opportunity for sharing information about your hobby or your cultural background. Photography, gardening, nutrition, cooking and sewing are just a few of the popular subjects waiting to be taught. The list is as long as your own imagination and ingenuity can make it. There are openings for non-accredited teachers in many other programs similar to those I have mentioned. Check them out through the Chamber of Commerce, state, city and county governments.

There are also opportunities to teach groups in your own home, a church or some rented building. If you have something to offer that the government feels is needed, there is a good chance you can get your program funded by the federal government.

TURNING FOUR TO SIX HOURS A WEEK INTO BIG PROFITS

A weekly newspaper columnist, Jacques C., started a cooking school as a sideline in one of the prosperous communities near his home. He picked a location convenient to all the wealthy people in that area and set up a school specializing in gourmet cooking. Jacques held the classes three nights a week and made a weekly charge of $25 to each of his students. With thirty or more regular students, he earned considerably more at the six-hour-a-week job than he did from his full-time position.

He specialized in gourmet dishes, wine and cocktail selections and attractive methods of serving.

Equipment and supplies needed for this business vary, depending on how elaborate you want to be in the beginning. You will need at least a good set of pots and pans, plastic plates, spoons and forks (for tasting) and food supplies.

Jacques gave out a typewritten sheet to all his students giving them a written description of the recipes used at each lesson. He taught in a room leased in a business building for $250 a month. Here he had to put in a refrigerator, stove and counter.

With good credit, such a business can be started for about $2,000. It can be done for much less if you teach in your home where you already have most of the equipment.

Cheryl M., a wife and mother of three, put out a small neatly printed booklet of pointers on how to stay attractive to your husband. She then set up classes on the same theme for a group of 20 to 30 women. The group later expanded to a point where she had to move into larger quarters. She gave a two-hour course two nights a week which lasted six weeks, and charged $10 for it. Her only expense was the cost of printing the booklets—$25 for her first 1,000. The sales of the booklets paid for future printing.

SIX RULES OF SUCCESSFUL TEACHING

1. Be thoroughly aware of the learning absorption rate of the students you are teaching—aware of individual rates as much as possible.

2. Know the motivation of each student—why he or she wants to learn the subject matter—the student's inner drive for this skill or information.

3. Insist on a teaching plan of student involvement. Bear in mind the key fact: people learn by doing.

4. Constantly tie in the students' accumulated experience with the new learning. The past experience is the anchor for the new. It is sometimes known as "related learning."

5. Vary the teaching methods widely; i.e., lecture, problem solving, group activity, assignment, role playing, simulation, audiovisual, feedback. Include role switching where students become the instructors, lead questions, association problems where you associate their learning with real problems. Field observation where they see the new learning in action is very important.

6. Supply the students with immediate and constant feedback on their performance. Use praise lavishly—most people need it. This is B.F. Skinner's philosophy and is now widely used in industry.

HIDDEN OPPORTUNITIES AMONG ALL AGES

We often think of teaching as something done only by people between the ages of 20 and 65, but there are opportunities in this field for every age group.

There are some situations where it is better to have a high school student than an adult as a teacher and in some cases, grade school youngsters are best qualified. Jon R., a 16-year-old, lived in a townhouse complex where there was a large swimming pool. Jon noticed that a number of rather small children who lived in the townhouses never went near the water.

He got acquainted with the parents of two youngsters—three and five years of age—and asked them if he could teach the children to swim. The parents consented, and Jon had the start of a swimming class that grew to several students. He charged $2 an hour for his lessons and made $400 during the summer months.

Dan G., 43 years of age, teaches swimming the year round at a country club, making about $800 a month. In a situation such as this there is no need for an investment, since all the equipment is furnished.

If you have a pool in your own yard, you may want to teach right there. In this case you will need to spend from $60 to $100 for insurance and about $55 for a year's supply of chlorine. You can paint indicators of the different depths on the pool yourself with about $1.25 worth of paint.

Tennis is another sport taught by teenagers and adults as well. The younger teachers usually get from $7 to $8 an hour. A real pro can make an excellent income from this all year round. Jay T. charged only $8 a lesson. A conservative day for him brought as much as $96.

George R., an insurance adjuster, spent his weekends and some evenings teaching at a private club. He was a top pro and got as much as $20 a lesson.

Two little girls, Lena J., 12 years old, and June F., 13, organized classes in their neighborhood letting their students pay whatever they wanted to. Lena taught modern jazz and ballet, and June taught gymnastics. They put a plate by the door for student donations. Both girls averaged between $10 and $15 for a two-hour lesson.

On the other hand, a senior citizen is far better suited to teaching any subject where his or her experience outshines anyone else in the field. There are many senior citizens teaching and counseling in business areas where their extensive experience is invaluable.

TUTORING THE SLOW LEARNER

There was a time when only the very wealthy could afford a tutor or a governess. Today there are federally funded programs geared to individual instruction, making it possible for people of all income levels to have tutoring when necessary.

Probably one of the most expansive tutoring endeavors was Dr. Frank Lauback's "Each One Teach One" program for the illiterate in India. Several thousand illiterates learned to read through this project.

There is almost as great a need for this in our country among our illiterate. This type of program can be financed by government grants. If you think you have the ability and interest necessary for this, research Dr. Lauback's program through your local library and plan a similar one for the illiterate sections of our country. Staff members of local antipoverty agencies in your vicinity can help you prepare the necessary proposal for a grant, or direct you to someone you can engage to do it for a fee.

There are numerous opportunities all around you, too, for individual tutoring. If you are an accredited teacher, you can find your students through the schools. If not, you may locate them through a classified ad, through business organizations, clubs and government agencies or any referral program working extensively with people in all walks of life.

Joyce C. was a retired teacher who discovered an opportunity to work as a teacher of homebound children for the school where she once taught. The school sent her to the homes of children who were unable to attend school because they were ill or temporarily handicapped in some way. She received $20 an hour for this work.

Regular tutoring by non-accredited teachers brings anywhere from $5 to $10 an hour. If you have the necessary experience, don't let the lack of a degree deter you from going into this field. There are many opportunities for the experienced but non-accredited individual.

SPANISH IMMIGRANT DEVELOPS SIMPLIFIED METHOD
FOR TEACHING LANGUAGE

Anita Ramos de Schaff emigrated from Spain to the United States when she was 13 years of age. She had considerable difficulty with our language and, because of her inability to communicate in English, was labeled a retarded person. Consequently, she determined someday to develop a simple learning method for others like herself who needed to master a foreign language.

Through her persistent efforts in this direction she was successful in getting a full-tuition language scholarship to Brown University. She was the first woman to receive such a scholarship. To get through college she worked at almost any job she could find—in stores, factories, radio shops, as a bobbin girl in a weaving factory and even as a production manager for a precision tooling company.

Anita never never gave up her goal to simplify language instruction. She finally perfected the "Common Sense Method" (CSM) of teaching languages and wrote several books on the subject. Using this method students do not have to conjugate verbs: they merely learn six rules which enable them to construct 14 tenses. They do not have to memorize 84 different verb endings either—only four. Her whole program is based on emphasizing similarities in language experience instead of differences in languages.

When local newspaper stories about her work brought requests for language lessons, she decided to start teaching in her home once or twice a week. As the word got around that her students were learning a foreign language in 17 to 20 lessons with instant vocabularies of 6,000 words, her popularity grew. In one year's time the once or twice weekly classes grew to daily classes with 150 students every month. Today people come to her from all over the United States: straight A students who couldn't learn a language after four years of traditional classes, ambassadors, diplomats and many others. She has students from all walks of life—all she can handle and more waiting.

Teaching a foreign language with this method requires the purchase of three books at a cost of $10, six tapes costing $10 each, and the lessons costing $150, making a total cost of $220.

The minimum daily income for 3½ hours of work is $20, and

can be $30 or more working from three to six hours a day.

An expert such as Mrs. Schaff can make as much as $75 in half an hour.

HOW TO OPEN DOORS TO SKILLS TRAINING OPPORTUNITIES

There is a great deal of government money available for experimental demonstration projects. This is especially true in the field of skills training. Grants for several thousand dollars for this type project can be obtained, depending on the program.

There is a particular interest in finding ways to reach and train the high school dropout. In one southwestern city alone there were between 2,000 and 3,000 high school dropouts from a single school district in one year. If you have an idea for a workable training program for dropouts, write a proposal and submit it to the Department of Health, Education and Welfare or the Office of Education in Washington, D.C. The proposal would be for an Experimental Demonstration program.

You should also go to the high school district in your area and tell their officials that you have an idea you know will provide a good training program for dropouts, and ask that they identify these people for you. You will have to seek out the young people and apply for the funds yourself.

You can go, also, to a skills training center and find out how much it costs to train people there. You will want to discover the interests of these young dropouts and develop your program around that. You can offer to teach many of the usual skills such as automotive, welding, cooking, meat cutting, clerical, nurses' aide and sales cashier. If you have any of these skills or new ideas of your own, you may find this field worth exploring.

MUSICAL INSTRUMENT TEACHING

If you are accomplished in playing a musical instrument and have a knack for teaching others your skill, this can be a lucrative and satisfying profession for you.

Mary Beth Sells started playing piano when she was four years old. Later, when she was working as a secretary, she began teaching piano to the children of her friends. Her success with these children brought other students and soon she had a sizeable group—all she could handle. This required no investment. She charged $5 a student.

Mary L., a retired teacher, started with two or three piano students and very shortly was busy six hours a day six days a week, earning $30 or more daily.

Roger Ricketts first studied accordian at age seven and played drums with a school band in fourth grade. In high school his music teacher, recognizing his ability, started Ricketts teaching accordian to fellow students. He worked with only one beginner at first, then slowly built his group of students to twenty or thirty. In a short time he progressed to a point where he could teach anyone beginner to advanced techniques.

When the school couldn't pay him adequately for the number of students he had acquired, he went on his own. A stroke of luck enabled him to take over a deserted business operation. Here, with only two chairs, a music stand and his own personal music and instrument, he set up a studio for accordian lessons. Later he taught drum students, setting that section up with a pair of drumsticks and a board. Since then he has added guitar and piano teachers to his staff and later began teaching piano himself. Ricketts said he would never have made it through college if it had not been for his music. It financed him through all four years.

The hourly charge for these lessons is $8. The business can be started on very little capital—practically nothing if you have your own music and instrument. You can ask your students to buy their own books.

NEW METHODS OF TEACHING OFFICE SKILLS

Secretarial skills are rapidly becoming automated along with everything else in this machine-oriented world. The latest trend seems to be to Word Processing. Written communications are produced at top speed by WP accurately, with little effort and at low cost. This is accomplished by the combined use of correct procedures, automated equipment and properly trained personnel. Two types of equipment involved in WP are automatic typing and dictating. The vendor of the machinery does the training.

Word Processing is a magnetic tape Selectric typewriter process. The machine can type 175 words a minute without error. The boss telephones in his message through the use of equipment known as the "Dictation Tank." Trained clerical personnel develop his letters, leaving his secretary free to function in an administrative capacity.

A number of the larger companies throughout the country are beginning to use WP. This eliminates much of the need for clerical skills amd means secretaries will be doing other things.

One eastern company using Word Processing entirely has found it streamlines written communications. A vice president of the company indicated that the new program has increased their utilization of personnel.

"We have been able to use a number of our former secretaries for other types of work," he said. "It has opened our eyes to many unknown sources of talent, and secretaries are now performing numerous tasks previously handled only by the managerial staff."

For more detailed information on this innovation in office procedures, read some of the articles on the subject in the magazine, *Modern Office Procedures.*

To keep up with the modern trend, secretarial training must take on new dimensions.

June E., a secretarial supervisor in an insurance firm, had the right idea when she set up special classes in her home for clerical employees. June didn't teach shorthand and typing; instead she taught some of the extra things she felt a good secretary should know. Her classes emphasized communicating with and entertaining board members on their level, finesse in handling people, motivation and additional skills in library research and guidelines for public speaking. When June started her classes it was to help the women in her company prepare for something better. Her theory was that secretaries, who were in a position to learn a great deal about the firms for which they work, should equip themselves for possible executive job openings. The classes were so successful that secretaries from other companies wanted to take them. June was able to charge $25 a course. There was no cost in setting up the classes. She built this part-time activity to a point where she was making $500 a month from it, working only three nights a week.

Today, with increasing automation, this type of training seems quite important.

INSTRUCTIONS IN MAKING UNUSUAL CRAFTS

The best approach to teaching crafts classes is to work with a hobby shop. If you have the ability to teach a skill to others, there are a number of hobby shops who will give you an opportunity to conduct classes in their stores at night. Many of these businesses are interested only in promoting the materials in their shop through such classes, so the whole fee can go the the teacher.

Vonda's Trunks and Treasures in Scottsdale, Arizona, which offers instruction in making unusual crafts, was started when Vonda Jessup wanted to develop a business which would provide a new interest for her mother after her father's death.

She started with $200 capital and leased a small house where she taught the art of refurbishing antique trunks and other crafts, selling the crafts as well. Vonda put all the money back into the business until it grew to a self-supporting operation—from the little house to a 5,000 square foot building with nine employees.

She charges $3 for all craft classes except trunk refurbishing, which is $5 a lesson with some materials furnished. Vonda teaches the trunk classes, showing her students how to totally redo these old trunks, cleaning them, sanding them, re-painting, designing and lining them.

To be a success in this field, Vonda says, you need a wild imagination because you have to come up with new ideas all the time. The base of the business is the retail craft shop, but the classes play an important part in the business: 50 or more students participate every week.

ENGLISH INSTRUCTION FOR NEWCOMERS TO THE U.S.

If you are bilingual you should be ideally suited to teaching English to those who speak your language, especially if you use the proper teaching technique.

Anita Ramos de Schaff, mentioned earlier in this chapter, recommends not teaching foreigners grammar rules, but teaching them phonetically instead. There are several books on the market now that advocate this method, but Mrs. Schaff says all or most of them use the wrong phonetic sound in some instances—the use of "i" for example. "I" is long "e" in Spanish. When "i" is used in the spelling of a word, a Spanish person will say it as though it were a long "e."

In any profession, the one who provides the best service gets the most business. English instruction is no exception to this rule. If you have the necessary background—the ability to speak English and at least one other language accurately and the proper technique—there are many students waiting for you.

Go to the State Department and the Office of Immigration for prospective students. Check also with your Chamber of Commerce for names and meeting places of clubs oriented to various nationalities. You should be able to find all the students you can handle.

The average hourly rates for this work are about the same as for teaching foreign languages.

TEACHING THE UNUSUAL IN SEWING OPPORTUNITIES

Elsie L., a housewife and mother, made costumes for her young son and daughter for a school play. They were so superb that the mothers of other children asked her to teach them the technique. Soon word got around that she not only was teaching her neighbors how to put costumes together quickly and economically but teaching them authenticity in design as well.

A director from one of the local theatre groups saw the results of her work and asked Elsie to show members of his cast how to make authentic costumes for their parts. For this assignment she was paid $10 apiece from twenty performers—a total of $200 for a few hours' work.

This encouraged her to go into the business professionally. She started contacting other theatre groups, school drama classes and prospective brides. To the latter she offered classes to teach bridesmaids how to make their own high-fashion dresses inexpensively.

In a short time she built a steady business in this specialty field, and students came to her whenever they had a need for the unusual—a one-time outfit. She taught them how to make inexpensive material look expensive. In less than six months she was making from $700 to $1,000 a month. She had no investment because she already had a sewing machine, and her students bought their own materials and supplies.

A NEW APPROACH TO THE FIELD OF MECHANICS

Many high schools have classes in auto mechanics as do a number of skills training centers. Usually, however, the students are men, and the classes are not geared to the needs of the average woman. Women often get "taken" by unscrupulous auto mechanics because of their ignorance. As a consequence, a few farsighted mechanics have started teaching classes especially for women, but this approach is still so new the field is wide open.

Al J. was working as a service station attendant and making only an average income when he discovered how little most of his female customers knew about cars.

The more he thought about it the more he realized the need for some kind of instruction along these lines, and he started feeling out some of his customers. He discovered most of them were tired of being cheated and were eager to learn more about their cars. When he proposed a special class for them, sixteen women signed up immediately. He charged them $30 each for four weeks, two nights a week. The class was so successful he had another group waiting when this first course was completed. Before a year was up he had all the students he could handle and more waiting, so he quit his job and worked only at this. Many months he made $1,200 or more, teaching only about twenty hours a week.

He had no investment since he taught the classes in his own carport and he had his own tools.

Frequently his students repaired cars under his direction: this provided additional income. These people paid for their own parts, so no investment was required. He didn't need to keep any parts on hand, because he could pick up anything he needed for a job from the auto parts supply houses nearby.

TEACHING PHYSICAL EDUCATION
THROUGH UNTAPPED SOURCES

Many municipal parks and recreation departments hire physical education teachers, on a part-time basis. The pay is in the neighborhood of $3.50 an hour. This is an excellent opportunity to gain experience in the field.

For the physical education teacher who would like to develop his or her own group there are many untapped sources for students. Country clubs, mobile home parks, adult living complexes and adult communities are just a few of the areas where the surface has barely been scratched in this field. Some adult communities have classes taught by volunteers in the area but as these communities grow in size, the need for professional physical education teachers increases.

There are many areas in this field where private students are available and teachers get anywhere from $2 to $10 an hour, depending upon their background and skill.

In most cases no investment is required, since equipped facilities are available in many of these communities.

FORMER MODEL TEACHES WOMEN
TO MAKE THEIR OWN COSMETICS

Marina Goldie was a high fashion model first in Washington, D.C., then New York City and in San Francisco when she started giving herself special skin care. Later she began giving these treatments to friends, continuing with her modeling at the same time. Because of her unique approach to the profession and the excellent results of her work, she soon was receiving pay for this service. As her reputation became known as a skin care specialist, she developed a wealthy clientele and began beauty consultant work, teaching others how to make the cosmetics she uses.

Marina taught these women how to make these cosmetics using food products from their own kitchens. She showed them how to manipulate the skin with their hands without the use of electricity and how to benefit from the use of herbs. She charged from $10 to $12 an hour with an additional $3 to $5 charge for makeup.

One would need to go to a cosmetic school and become a professional beautician before entering this profession. You can then start teaching with little or no investment.

OFFERING UNIQUE CLASSES IN HOME MANAGEMENT

Carol A., a housewife, contacted officers of sororities, women's church groups and women's clubs, making arrangements to present her program to the members at their regular meetings. Through these presentations she interested several women in coming to her home for special classes in home management.

Carol taught them simplicity in clothing, drapery and furnishings styles, and them how, in only 26 minutes a day, to keep their houses clean and orderly. She had worked out this method in her own home through trial and error.

These classes, for which she charged $2 a person, grew so much in popularity that she began holding them in the Women's Club with as many as 100 people attending.

For the trained home economists there are a variety of opportunities for teaching through universities and community colleges. The University of Arizona Extension Service works with a group of home economists who instruct women informally on money management, consumer buying and other home management matters. One time, for example, they gave instructions on how to change the oil filter in a car. The home economists brought a car into the school auditorium where they gave a demonstration. These instructors work with homemaker clubs—neighborhood groups—who send representatives to the classes.

One untapped source of students is mothers of preschool children. These women don't have the usual contacts mothers of school-age children have and are often bypassed entirely. Investigate methods for finding these mothers. You can secure many names through child nurseries or by going door-to-door. You can also leave brochures in the offices of pediatricians and in child-care clinics. This is virgin territory from which you can develop as large a group of students as you wish.

CONDUCTING BUSINESS MANAGEMENT SEMINARS

Jerry W., a former insurance salesman, contacted companies involved in direct or commission sales such as insurance, real estate and door-to-door cosmetics firms. He succeeded in getting these firms to cosponsor his business management seminars, then set up meetings to inform their sales forces of the benefits they would derive from his motivation courses.

He sold them a one-year program for $38 per person with a seminar every other month with two speakers each time. The sessions were held from 7:30 to 10:00 PM in a room rented from one of the convention-oriented hotels in his city. He kept his overhead down by shopping around for the best rental price at a prestige location and by using speakers, wherever possible, who were already coming to that area. This cut down considerably on traveling and lodging costs which Jerry paid in addition to the speaker's fee of $200 to $500. Whenever possible he engaged local speakers who had appeal as outstanding leaders in the community. Whenever his speakers were authors of books, he made additional money from the sale of these books, which he bought at the author's cost. Jerry always had 1,000 to 3,000 people taking these seminars, and would never present one for less than 1,000 participants.

TEACHING TIPS FOR AUDIO VISUAL

A study of visual aids and their benefits as memory aids revealed that people who remember only 21 percent of what they are taught will, with a visual aid, remember 78 percent. Most people learn more easily if there is something in the learning process with which they can identify. Many people have difficulty learning in certain areas where they have had no experience and, consequently, no reality. For example, if you didn't even know there were other countries, you would be unable to recognize that a franc is a piece of money in France just as a dollar bill is money in the United States.

Using visual aids in teaching overcomes much of this handicap because the students can see what they are studying as well as hear the instruction.

Roy Amrein, a chiropractor, has been teaching business groups motivation, sales techniques and good business practices through the use of visual aids for several years. One of the many courses he has conducted was for the sales force and staff members of a large Chevrolet dealer in his city. He held the classes once a week and received $200 a month for his services.

Dr. Amrein says the best way to get some such classes started is to go to groups interested in improving their income-earning ability. Community colleges are often interested in offering a wide variety of classes to the general public. Numerous businesses feel the need for classes in motivation and sales techniques among their employees. If you have something to offer these organizations and firms and are looking for a more effective way to put it across, visual aids may be your answer.

In seeking students, start with the smaller businesses and move into the big industries once you are better established.

For a simple beginning you will need an overhead projector. A used one will cost about $75 and a new one approximately $300. Another $12 or $15 will buy clear plastic rolls to write on—enough to make 50 slides—and a package of marking pencils. That is all you will need as a starter; most businesses will furnish room space.

HOW TO GET ALL THE STUDENTS YOU WANT

There are people wanting to learn almost any subject that can be taught, but they need to know where they can get this instruction. It is up to you, then, to make your services known where it will mean the most. If you are teaching real estate, go to all the real estate firms and make your services known. The same goes for insurance companies or other businesses.

A former insurance salesperson, Geraldine A., did this, contacting insurance companies all through her area. She made $50 an hour teaching fire rating.

Mark T. makes $40,000 in a single weekend teaching real estate seminars.

Both of these people got their students by door-to-door contact with the firms involved in the type of business that fit their particular area.

Schools are constantly looking for teachers. Many of them don't require certification. Simple classified ads costing from $3 to $10 are frequently the best way to start.

12

Offering Unusual Yet Much Needed Services

Society moves at such a rapid pace these days that people generally are working against time every day of their lives. Few of us have the needed hours to do all the extra chores confronting us daily, so we employ others to do much of what we did as a matter of course a few years ago. This opens the door to the enterprising individual who has a service to offer busy people for a fee. If you have the talent, or in many cases, just the desire to provide a service that saves time for others, you have a moneymaker.

One of the many advantages to starting a service business is that as a rule, such a business can be operated with little or no capital. It also brings in good money, especially if the service is something wanted and needed by a lot of people. You should take stock of the situation in your community—discover its needs and desires—then explore your own abilities and gear them to the demand. The opportunities are waiting—many of them right at your doorstep.

DISCOVERING THE NEEDS AND ALIGNING THEM WITH YOUR ABILITIES

The first place to look for needed services is in your own environment. What are some of the things you would be willing to pay to have done if you had the extra money? Talk with friends and neighbors to discover other services needed which are not adequately supplied. You can expand your survey by talking with members of organizations to which you belong and to business people with whom you trade.

Once you have compiled a comprehensive list of needs your next step is to assess your own abilities and how they fit the needs.

When you are assessing your abilities don't overlook such things as the ability to relate to people and a desire to help.

Joyce W., a housewife, had no professional or skill training and felt somewhat inadequate around her talented friends; then she discovered a much-needed service she could give them. Frequently, in their conversations with her, they mentioned errands they should have run that day but hadn't done because they ran out of time. Joyce realized time was something she had plenty of, so she began running errands for her busy friends. She started doing grocery shopping for two or three neighbors at a time—doing her own then, too. She made trips to the post office, drug store, health food store or whatever. As her customers grew in number she organized her various projects so she could handle errands for several people on one trip and incorporate her own errands into that same time space. She charged an hourly rate of $2 for the service and made as much as $10 an hour. Her only expense was the cost of operating her car.

UNIQUE SERVICE BECOMES BIG BUSINESS FOR OLDER COUPLE

John and Sarah P., a retired couple, had a big empty, lonely house when their seven children grew up and left home. They missed the round of activities that had taken place in that home for so many years and the company of people generally. While the children were still with them John and Sarah used to enjoy playing cards with other parents frequently. This, too, had stopped when friends moved to other areas or became involved in new activities. As they both realized what a vacuum all this had left in their lives they wondered if there were not a lot of other couples in the same situation. They ran the following classified ad steadily for a few weeks at a total cost of under $50: "WANTED: Card-playing couples and individuals looking for partners and a place to play. We have the space and we will supply the partners. For more details call John or Sarah, 222-3456." They were flooded with calls and soon had a house full of card-playing clients. They charged a fee of $3 a person or $5 a couple, making as much as $100 a day at times and having a lot of fun in the process.

PROVIDING TEMPORARY HOME WORKERS

Many people are looking for qualified people to take care of invalids or convalescents in their home. This is a very lucrative business and is especially suited to a retired nurse or someone with this type of training or experience.

When my mother was ill and unable to care for herself I needed a competent person to care for her until I could work out a satisfactory permanent arrangement. There was one agency in our city offering qualified and fully trained help for this kind of sevice. It was the only place that guaranteed the quality of the service and the qualifications of those they sent to your home. They charged a minimum of $70 a 40-hour week, but the customer had complete assurance of satisfactory service. It was worth the price because competent help for invalids and convalescents in your own home is difficult to find.

I tried some of the less expensive help with no success. There is a big market waiting for the professional firm providing guaranteed satisfaction in this area.

The only investment is the cost of office rent and upkeep. As the business grows, more office staff will be required, but that can be financed by the business itself.

OFFERING SPECIAL BUS SERVICE FOR THE ELDERLY

There are many elderly people who no longer drive their cars and who are totally dependent upon busy relatives or friends to do their shopping for them. A number of these people are confined to their homes because of this transportation problem and never have a chance to buy anything for themselves. My mother suffered from this handicap because she never drove a car—after my father's death, her independent transportation was taken away completely. She had more opportunity than many older people because I did take her whenever I could, but it was not enough to satisfy all her needs. I was busy on a full-time, eight-to-five job, along with my writing and other after-hours activities. I tried to find other transportation for her, but was successful only to a limited degree.

If someone had offered me a special bus service for taking my mother shopping and to the doctor, I would have subscribed immediately. This has been offered in some areas and has proved highly profitable.

HOW ONE WOMAN EARNED GOOD MONEY
OFFERING THIS SERVICE

Opal T., a practical nurse, visited several senior citizen clubs in her city, went to adult communities and nursing homes and ran a classified ad in the newspaper to find elderly clients needing special transportation services. She purchased a good used Volkswagen bus for about $1,500, financing most of the cost. She then worked out a schedule whereby she could pick up nine elderly people along a particular route and take them shopping. On certain days she dropped some of her passengers at doctors' offices or clinics where they had appointments. Charging $4 a person, she took in as much as $70 in a day.

DOING RESEARCH FOR GOVERNMENT OFFICES AND BUSINESSES

There are many projects both in government and private business that require extensive research before they can be launched. This is a wide open field for the person skilled in uncovering special data. Non-fiction writers often have an excellent background for this most productive sideline.

Government grants are available to individuals and firms having a service—particularly in the field of training the disadvantaged—that fills a community need. To adequately present this need and the method for handling it, a great deal of research is usually needed. Often those who wish to apply for the grant are not adequately familiar with its requirements or don't have the time to research the project. This is where the freelance research specialist can find much of his business.

Some research specialists, such as Brad C., owner and publisher of a weekly newspaper, do special research jobs for government agencies or businesses. Brad took his first such job with an anti-poverty agency needing to set up a reference library for the general use of its staff. He took a leave of absence from his newspaper job for two months and did special research on poverty conditions and workable solutions. Brad continued to act in an advisory capacity to his newspaper staff during this period, but gave most of his daytime hours to the research activity. This first project, which paid him $50 a day, opened the door to many similar jobs in the future, most of which he was able to handle while still operating his weekly newspaper. As he built his reputation in this area, his daily fee increased.

A considerable amount of government money is being allocated to research these days. If you would like more information on how to get into this field, write to the Office of Economic Opportunity, 1200 19th Street, N.W., Washington, D.C. 20206.

PROVIDING MAILING LISTS FOR BUSINESSES

There are retail merchandisers in most communities who do some of their advertising through direct mail contacts. These are ready customers for special mailing lists. You can assemble a variety of lists for various specialty businesses by merely reading daily newspapers and copying names and address from stories. There will be stories about weddings, engagements, business successes and many other things. If the individual's address isn't given, find a city directory and look it up there. Offer the lists you compile to retail stores or service agencies in your city. Individuals and businesses selling merchandise by mail order throughout the country are always in the market for good mailing lists.

Calvin R. sold an information report about government services by mail order. He advertised his product by placing small classified ads in a few nationally circulated magazines, and developed an extensive mailing list as well as sales for his report. He began renting this list to other businesses after advertising it in *Direct Marketing*. It proved an excellent sideline to his mail order operation. His initial advertising costs were under $100 and his list rental fees paid for future ads. He charged rental fees from $25 to $50 per thousand names for one-time use only.

PERFORMING A SPECIAL GIFT SERVICE

Reva J., a bookkeeper for a produce company, had a young granddaughter who was confined to the hospital for three weeks. Reva wanted to make her stay more pleasant. She went to variety stores in her area and picked out all kinds of small gift items, most of which cost considerably under a dollar. These she gift-wrapped individually. Every day for the three-week period she put a package in the mail on her way to work.

Her grandchild was so thrilled with the daily gifts that Reva overflowed with enthusiasm for her project. Soon word got around about it and people began offering to pay a fee if she would do the same for ill members of their families. She found it such a delightful occupation that she began advertising in the local newspaper through the classified section and later in national publications.

Her only investment was the advertising; this was paid for by the fees of those friends who were her first clients. Her customers paid for the gift items and postage in addition to her $2 fee for mailing. She turned all her fees back into the business at the beginning and, with this money, started purchasing the gift items herself at wholesale prices to sell to her customers at a 100 percent mark-up. This brought her additional income. In a few months she was earning from $200 to $300 extra spending money each month.

TEN UNIQUE APPROACHES TO A WOMEN'S EXCHANGE

Women's Exchanges usually are shops that sell handmade items for women on a consignment basis. Some do very well, being able to operate on low capital because of no product investment. They might, however, do even better with a few innovations. First of all, they should change the name to People's Exchange and sell merchandise from men as well as women.

Here are some innovations that can add considerably to the income and general appeal of such a shop:

1. Promote custom-made dresses and suits for seamstresses and tailors for a percentage of their charges.

2. Have crafts people making some of their products in the shop so customers can watch the process.

3. Promote services as well as products.

4. Display some of the crafts from your shop in public buildings such as bank or office building lobbies.

5. Have a booth at a crafts fair.

6. Hold crafts classes in your shop.

7. Put on a gala sidewalk display once a month.

8. Offer crafts or other merchandise showings in restaurants the same way fashions are modeled for the entertainment of the customers.

9. Put on a fund-raising campaign dividing the profits between the charity, the crafts people and the store.

10. Act as a distributor for door-to-door sales of items carried in your store.

OFFERING SOMETHING DIFFERENT IN HOME DELIVERY

Delivery service is a thing of the past in a number of business operations today, but it is still needed, particularly for purchases in heavy items.

Probably one type of business which needs this service most is hardware. For the customer who doesn't own a pickup truck it is difficult to take some of these items home.

You can purchase a good used truck for $1,000 or less. Then you should paint a big sign on each side which says: DELIVERY SERVICE TO YOUR HOME. Park your truck outside a hardware store or large furniture warehouse where delivery service isn't available and wait for customers. To assure yourself of steady business you can make arrangements to pay the stores a small percentage for jobs referred to you.

Another excellent place to find customers for home delivery service is a park and swaps or flea markets. You will have to make your services known, but there will be plenty of customers needing transportation for all their purchases in any of these places. Your charges will have to vary depending on distances and amount of merchandise delivered.

I EARNED GOOD MONEY SELLING "WE APPROVE" SERVICE

Cecil and Pearl E. grew weary of trying to find reliable service people when they were new in town. They couldn't even find anyone capable of advising them in this area. Cecil was an insurance salesman but decided to start a special referral service on the side so others wouldn't have the same problems he was encountering. Most of his insurance sales work was at night, giving him considerable free time during the day to explore the possibilities of this new venture. He began checking various services in the city: plumbers, electricians, auto mechanics, landscape artists and a wide variety of repair specialists.

He and Pearl were living in an old house in a business-zoned area. They turned part of this into office space. They hired me to sell memberships to the businesses they had already checked and found reliable. Their operation was called "We Approve." I was instructed to sell memberships only to firms and individuals who had passed their careful scrutiny. We charged each member firm a special fee, then advertised our service and telephone number extensively through the newspapers, by radio and special fliers and through distribution of our business cards. Our ads encouraged people to call for our approval when they needed a service.

The only investment was for advertising; this came to approximately $500 in the beginning. My commission came out of the membership fees, and I collected that amount as a down payment on the membership. The commissions were never less than $200 a week; the total intake of the business nearly tripled that.

THE SECRETS OF SUCCESSFUL LECTURE TOURS

The first and most essential ingredient for successful lecture tours is the right subject matter. You must choose a subject with wide general appeal. The most successful lectures have been about self-improvement.

Once you have selected a subject that is meaningful to the general public in all parts of the country, you must then do whatever is necessary to fully inform yourself on this subject. The ideal situation is lecturing on a popular subject in which you are already an expert. But this is not an absolute essential, because anyone can become informed if he or she has the persistence and determination to study and learn thoroughly. Never attempt lecturing on half knowledge. Choose the right subject and learn every aspect of it.

I think the most successful participants in lecture tours are those who become a part of a specific lecture circuit which is already popular. This gives you some backing in the early stages, but it does not eliminate the necessity for you to do your own promoting. This you must do always unless you are among the few who have been successful in finding and employing a successful lecture promoter. This is an exception to the rule, however; most lecturers doing successful tours are promoting their own speaking schedules. They do this through extensive mail-outs to professional groups all over the country that are interested in self-improvement. Sales organizations and business executives are good prospects.

It isn't necessary to become part of an already established lecture tour circuit. You can develop your own by acquiring lists of promotional-type business organizations throughout the country and sending professional promotion material to them. You should have a qualified advertising agency put together a good mailing brochure and other descriptive material about you and your subject.

It is helpful to have tapes of lectures you have given before groups and letters of appreciation from some of these organizations. To accumulate this type of promotional material, you may find it necessary to do some free lecturing in your own community at first.

LECTURING BECOMES TOP MONEY MAKER
FOR FORMER SECRETARY

Merlyn Cundiff had been a secretary for a number of years when she became interested in lecturing and began preparing herself on the side for this profession. During many of her years as a secretary she had a boss who taught her all the facets of his operation; there she developed a basic knowledge of business and people. What she learned from him and through her own determination to improve has been invaluable in developing her own successful venture.

In her youth she suffered from a severe physical handicap—stuttering—and she was always a timid person who would have been petrified at the thought of speaking before an audience.

She overcame this only because she was a totally determined person with definite purposes and goals.

"I wanted certain things out of life," she said. "I wanted professional prestige and income and was eager to travel to different parts of the world. And I think what I wanted most of all was an opportunity to help other people."

She started taking a self-improvement course given by Cavett Robert and demonstrated so much potential in these classes she was asked to consider becoming a circuit lecturer. When she finally decided to do this she left her secretarial position and made this her full-time profession.

She is author of the book, *Kinesics*, and has lectured in 17 countries on this subject—the science of nonverbal communication.

In a short five years she has built a quarter of a million dollar business speaking to sales managers, business executives and to more than 200 convention groups a year. She credits her success to association with people whose qualities she admires and respects and to positive thinking about life in general. Her financial success is above-average for this type of work, but she says an average income should be from $35,000 to $50,000 a year.

Merlyn doesn't want anyone to think it is an easy route. "It's a lot of work," she warns. It is not unusual for her to work 18 hours a day, seven days a week.

"But there are many rewards," she adds, "and I like my work, mainly because I like people."

PERFORMING A PROFESSIONAL LISTENING SERVICE

Marcia N. was a housewife whose brother was a psychiatrist. He always told her that what most of his patients needed was not an expensive psychiatrist, but a good listener.

Marcia thought about this quite a bit and finally decided it was a service she could perform and do well. She put an ad in the classified section of the paper urging people to talk over their problems with her. Her brother sent a few clients to her and word-of-mouth advertising brought many more. She charged $10 an hour for the service.

OFFERING A CALL SERVICE FOR ELDERLY PEOPLE

Vera Y., a former secretary, grew bored with inactivity after her retirement and decided to offer a service to other lonely people.

She knew several families in her church and club groups who had elderly relatives living alone, and she offered to make regular calls at specified times to these people for a $15 monthly fee. She agreed, also, for an additional $5, to go to the house if, at any time, the client didn't answer her call. The understanding was that she would always be informed ahead of time if her client would not be at home for the regular call. Then she would arrange to call at another time.

Vera found several ready customers from these first contacts and advertised in the paper for additional ones.

PET SITTING SERVICE

A few years ago we had a Chihuahua dog that was difficult to take with us when we traveled and more difficult to leave at home. Finally, we found a dog sitter who came to our home and stayed with Bambi whenever we were gone. She was free to go and come as she pleased as long as she provided some company for the dog along with feeding and other necessary attention. We were willing to pay the same fee charged by the dog kennels because this service was so much more satisfactory. We had tried the kennel route once before, and Bambi didn't eat for several days. She would have died, probably, had we been gone any longer.

Many people take dogs with them when this isn't at all satisfactory because they have no one with whom to leave them. This means the pets have to stay in locked cars on the road or in strange houses or motels.

It is much more satisfactory to employ a dog sitter. If you like dogs and other pets, advertise your services in the local newspapers. I know you will find plenty of customers, especially during the vacation season.

Walter J. started a dog-walking service in a wealthy neighborhood of New York City. Within a year he had a $25,000 yearly income.

PROVIDING EMPLOYMENT SERVICE FOR BABY SITTERS

When Julie C. was in her junior year of high school she did a lot of babysitting to earn extra spending money. When she started her senior year her study load was too heavy for her to find the necessary extra time for babysitting. She still continued to get calls from all her former customers. When she had to refuse so often some asked if she could find them another sitter of equal dependability. Julie began inquiring about babysitters among her friends and one of them suggested she charge a small fee in exchange for finding them jobs. Since she needed extra money and couldn't take the time to babysit herself, she decided to follow this suggestion and began charging 75¢ per job secured.

When the calls for babysitters grew in number beyond the few girls she had on her list, Julie ran a classified ad in the paper for more babysitters of all ages. Soon she was placing older women as well as young girls and an occasional young man who wanted the extra money. Within a short time her babysitting employment service was bringing in as much as $100 some months.

PLANT SITTING FOR VACATIONERS

Janet S., a retired school teacher, lived with her widowed sister and, at times, they got on each other's nerves. Janet tried spending a few months out of the year living with her children when things got rough between the two of them. This didn't work perfectly either because she didn't fit that well into their family life.

Then one day a woman in her church told Janet they didn't know what they would do about all their plants and their beautiful yard while they were away on vacation. They were going to be gone a month, and she didn't know where to find a reliable person who would water all these things.

Janet asked if they would like to have her stay in their house during that time so she could water their plants and lawn regularly. The friend was delighted. This was the beginning of a whole new career for Janet.

She did the first job so well her friend recommended her to others who kept her busy, sometimes for several weeks at a time.

Then Janet decided she would like to see some of her children back east, but she preferred not to stay with them. She advertised this same service in an East Coast newspaper and got a "plant sitting" job that enabled her to spend a month near her children. All her expenses were paid and she received $50 a week in salary.

This worked out so satisfactorily she did it in other parts of the country where she wanted to visit. She managed to travel extensively this way six months out of the year, sometimes more. She spent the other months "plant sitting" in her home territory with a few weeks off here and there to spend with her sister.

MUSICIAN PUTS TALENTS TO WORK FOR COMMUNITY PROJECTS

Arda Reeves was a civil service employee at the Veterans Hospital in Denver, Colorado when she decided to put a musical group together and do benefits for the hospital. She was the mistress of ceremonies, soloist and dancer for the group.

Arda had spent considerable time in Hawaii where she learned hula dancing from the native girls, so she planned a Hawaiian special for her first benefit performance. Through the local musicians' union she secured the services of a Hawaiian band and brought in Hawaiian students from the university to dance for the event.

This successful benefit led to others and as her reputation became known, she received paid offers to put on benefit shows for a number of organizations. For a fee of anywhere from $25 to $100 an

evening she put on benefit performances for the Veterans of Foreign
Wars, the American Legion, Kiwanis Clubs, Women's Club, March of
Dimes, YMCA and YWCA.

She has purchased a used portable Italian organ for $300 to do
her own accompaniment. Over the past few years Arda has composed
both the lyrics and music for a number of songs. Her songs all have a
special message and have been sung by a number of local enter-
tainers.

SHOPPING FOR OTHERS WHILE TRAVELING

When my sister took a tour of six European countries a few
years ago, a few of her friends and I asked her to bring souvenirs
from every country. Usually when a person travels to another
country or to a different section of this country, there are people
asking them to bring something back from that area. Most of us
don't know friends or have relatives going to all the places where we
would like purchases made, and we wouldn't want to impose our
wishes on a stranger—unless that stranger did it for a fee.

If you are a salesperson who travels extensively in this country
or one who makes frequent excursions to other parts of the world,
shopping for others is an excellent way to pay at least part of your
expenses. Advertise in the local papers and in national publications if
you want to expand your clientele. State where you are going and
offer to purchase items desired for a small fee.

If you are purchasing from other countries, you will need to
know what the export limitations are. You may want to investigate the feasibility of mailing some of the merchandise from
the country directly to your client.

CONDUCTING GARAGE SALES

Garage sales bring in a lot of money as a rule, but they are a
great deal of work for the seller. I had a profitable garage sale about
two years ago, but if I had it to do over again, I'd be happy to pay
someone else a percentage of the take to do the work for me.

If this sort of thing appeals to you, advertise in the paper and go
door-to-door offering your services for a percentage—about 30
percent—of the profits. The door-to-door approach is the best
method, an it will bring you all the customers you can handle.

Weekends are the most productive times for these sales, and you can easily earn a couple of hundred dollars for two days' work every week you hold a sale.

FOSTER FAMILY CARE

Foster homes for children have been in existence for a number of years, and many families take children into their home under this plan.

If you are interested in providing a home for children of broken homes or for those who are in other problem situations, check with your local welfare agency about the correct procedure.

In recent years a program has been under way to provide foster homes for the aged as well as children. This program serves older people who cannot function on their own and who are in need of or wish the security of living with a family.

The rate of payment to foster families is usually established by the local agency for this program in accordance with the standards of the particular state in which it exists. Adequate payment to attract desirable families who will offer the right kind of care for these elderly people is emphasized. Check with the Old Age Assistance program in your community for the proper procedure if you wish to become a foster parent for the aged. You can locate the Old Age Assistance program through your welfare department. For more details on this program write to the U.S. Department of Health, Education and Welfare, Welfare Administration, Bureau of Family Services, Washington, D.C. 20201 and ask for the booklet, "Foster Family Care for the Aged," P.A. Report No. 56.

OPERATING A PERSONALIZED HOUSEHOLD MOVING SERVICE

The last two times I moved I paid friends of mine to move me rather than employ the services of a professional moving company. The first time I would have had to postpone my move two or three weeks before I could even get a professional company to move my furniture. I was able to secure the services of my friends immediately.

If you have a good-sized truck or can purchase one, advertise your service in the newspapers and get the word around to apartment house tenants and others who are likely to move fairly often.

I paid only $25 for my first move and about $50 the second time, but the fee can be much more than that and still be a savings for the average mover. If your rates are fair and your service tops, you will soon have all the customers you want from word-of-mouth advertising.

There is always a market for any good service offered at a fair and equitable price. All you have to do is make your service known, and you will be in business.

13

Top Pay, Small-Investment Opportunities in Sales

Sales work is one of the highest paid professions in the world, offering a wide variety of opportunities to the willing worker. Whether the economy is good or bad it is always possible for a good salesman to earn a better-than-average income.

For the salesman who knows how to sell "intangibles" or has the aptitude for learning this type of selling, insurance is one of the most profitable fields to enter. There are a number of first-rate insurance salesman whose annual earnings range well over a million dollars; many general insurance agents take in $1,500 or more monthly.

There are some excellent opportunities as well for those who prefer to sell tangible products. Real estate can be one of the biggest money-makers, and cosmetics, home products, jewelry, food supplements are just a few of the areas with high-income potential.

There are job opportunities and business opportunities in all types of sales work. There are door-to-door sales approaches, sales from referrals, party plans, established route sales and excellent opportunities to act as representatives of national companies supplying regular professional and business accounts. The conscientious and able salesperson not only earns a more-than-adequate income but he or she serves public needs as well.

HOW TO QUALIFY FOR LUCRATIVE OPENINGS

Experience is always the best teacher in any field. In sales work it is of the essence if you want to move to the top of the ladder. There are a number of schools for training sales personnel and many valuable seminars which are excellent for developing the self-confidence so necessary to successful selling. All this will help you qualify for the more lucrative sales opportunities, but the place you will learn the most is in the field doing the job.

The most difficult types of sales work offer the most effective experience—they prepare you for anything you might encounter. Door-to-door selling is probably the hardest type to master successfully and is, therefore, the greatest teacher.

The first hurdle here is overcoming the fear of confronting a lot of strangers at their own doorsteps. Sometimes the fear of this first encounter can be overcome only through sheer necessity or desperation.

This was the case with Ruth P., a housewife who purchased a kit and membership for selling a food supplement. She let everything sit in her house for two long years while she tried to muster the courage to go door-to-door with her merchandise.

Finally, after reading a number of success stories about others selling these same products, she decided if they could do it, she could too. She went to the distributor and, in her new-found enthusiasm, purchased $1,700 worth of merchandise. This she stacked high in the corner of her bedroom. Then she panicked, realizing she had spent all her savings on that stack of vitamins. For the next few nights she barely slept, then she decided it was time to stop worrying and start acting. She had the merchandise, and she needed the money, so there was nothing to do but start selling.

She did just that and found it so much easier than she had anticipated that her enthusiasm spread to others. Soon she was signing up distributors to work under her, as she continued to sell the products herself. Ruth developed confidence from doing and in a short time was finding new distributors everywhere she went. "I was walking down the street in Toronto, Canada one day," she said, "and started talking to a perfect stranger whom I invited to one of my sales meetings. The woman came to the meeting and later became one of my biggest distributors."

Today, Ruth works at her sales program in a somewhat leisurely fashion but makes as much as $800 or more in a month.

THREE SECRETS TO SURE SALES WITH ANY PRODUCT

Some of the country's most successful salesmen list three basic truths for successful selling.

1. Learn just what your prospective customer wants, then help him find the best way to get it.

2. The only way to get anybody to do what you want is to make him want to do it.

3. When you show anyone you can help *him* get what *he* wants, he will do just about anything to help *you* get what *you* want.

These simple rules, listed several years ago, are as true today as they were then.

Making someone want something doesn't mean doing a con job on him or selling him something that will boomerang later. Before Rule No. 2 comes Rule No. 1—finding out what your prospect wants. You can then help him actually fulfill that need. First you help him look for the thing he really wants, then help him realize what it is, and the third rule will automatically take care of itself.

Several years ago, when I was selling wholesale gift merchandise to retail stores in three states, frequently I would suggest to a customer in a small shop that he or she not buy something. If I knew that person was planning to purchase too many necklaces when bracelets were moving faster in that area, I encouraged him or her to cut back on the necklace order. I never lost money doing this because I gained the confidence of all my customers by helping them discover what they really wanted. Their repeat purchases more than paid for whatever initial loss occurred.

CONTACTS THAT BRING YOU CUSTOMERS

The good salesman finds contacts everywhere he or she goes—on the street corner as Ruth P. did, in the corner drug store, in the beauty shop, at your church, club or business organization. Prospective customers are everywhere you are. You need only to be aware and alert. Ruth found one of her distributors when she dialed a wrong number. A strange voice answered the telephone when she rang the number, and she soon discovered she had dialed incorrectly. Immediately she took advantage of the situation.

"I was going to say this to Mr. Jones," she said, "but since I have you on the line, I'll tell it to you."

Ruth told him all about her food supplement and the sales program it offers. At first he indicated no need for such a program, but then he became interested and decided to explore it further. Like the woman Ruth met on the street corner in Canada, this man also became a customer of hers and later one of her top distributors.

Jess H. was a sales representative for a large hotel corporation interested in convention business. He wanted to sell his hotel as the best location for a future convention: making the right contacts for this was essential.

The organization was holding a convention at another hotel this year. As Jess stood at the registration desk of that hotel waiting, a man approached the desk. The girl behind the counter said to Jess, "This is Mr. Wentwell coming in now."

Mr. Wentwell was the man Jess needed to see. After he completed his business at the desk, Jess stepped forward and introduced himself as sales representative for the Mark Ellington Hotel. Wentwell was curt at first, but Jess merely invited him for a relaxing swim and lunch at the Mark Ellington after the close of the convention. Jess' invitation was not accepted then but was when they met again the following day.

Jess took his guest to the pool and left him there to enjoy it at his own pace. He picked him up later for lunch, then took him to the airport. During their brief visit Jess got all the important contacts he needed in order to sell his hotel as next year's convention home, and secured the full support of his newly made friend. Jess was at the right place at the right time to make the necessary contacts. This resulted in $45,000 sale for his company.

SELDOM KNOWN SALES METHODS THAT WORK

Bart R. was a sales representative for a large manufacturing firm selling industrial products to farmers. He was commissioned by his company to sell a new concept in packaging to a large grain industry. His first contact was with a purchasing agent who responded negatively to the approach in the beginning. Bart broke through some of his objections by emphasizing the difference in cost involved, but realized he needed another contact before he'd have any chance to make the sale.

Rather than bluntly request an audience with someone else to discuss his product, Bart asked the purchasing agent questions about their present packaging which he knew the man couldn't answer. This led the purchasing agent to refer Bart to the firm's director of merchandising. Here Bart encountered another man who couldn't give the final answer either. Employing the same technique—asking questions this man couldn't answer—got him finally to the top decision-maker, to whom Bart eventually made his sale.

Before seeing this man, Bart asked for a tour of the plant. This enabled him to discover more of the problems and needs of their packaging system. He followed this with a thorough study of the situation.

His unique methods of questioning and his thorough study of problems and solutions has made Bart a top producer in his field. In five years he raised the annual volume in his territory approximately $500,000.

UNSOPHISTICATED SALES APPROACH OPENS DOORS

Justin M. sells vacuum cleaners door to door and makes $30,000 to $50,000 a year, plus many lavish bonuses such as trips to Hawaii, new cars, color TVs or any number of elaborate gifts. His rather corny approach contrasts sharply with the more sophisticated sales techniques generally taught today, but his sales volume indicates its workability.

He might say to Mrs. Kelly, "That's a good Italian name—Kelly." Sometimes he hints to an older woman that she looks almost young enough to be his daughter. There are times when he actually pleads for permission to enter the house, arguing that his boss is breathing down his neck and he hasn't made a demonstration all day. He'll offer to clean a carpet to demonstrate his product. After he cleans the rug he piles rows of dirt on the floor from his vacuum cleaner—a dramatic demonstration for the greater effectiveness of his machine over hers. Frequently he offers a special trade-in allowance "because I need the sale and you need my machine."

He'll follow this with a definite statement. "Talk this over with your husband, Mrs. Jones. Let him know about the trade-in and the 18 months to pay. I'll be back this evening so you can sign the contract."

His approach is so direct it's almost unbelievable, but for Justin and the company he represents, it opens a lot of doors and pocketbooks.

HOW TO SELL BIG ON SHORT HOURS

The most immediate sales approach to big money for short

hours is the party plan. Under this plan the distributor gets friends and acquaintances to give parties in their homes in return for special gifts, the values of which are determined by the volume of sales for the evening. In many of these party plan programs added income is provided by what is known as pyramid sales. The original distributor finds sales people to work under him or her, and the distributor gets a percentage of these additional profits. It is possible to make from $30,000 to $40,000 a year through this type of sales work with little or no investment in the beginning.

Insurance offers another opportunity for big sales on short hours, but this situation cannot be developed overnight. It comes from writing a number of policy renewals which need to be built up over a period of a few years as a rule. Once these are established, it is possible to almost retire and still maintain a high standard of living.

Gil W. sold a hospitalization plan which gave 5 percent for renewals, and he sold enough policies in four years to retire with a steady income of $50,000 a year. Gil had only to work one or two months out of each year to keep this level of income flowing in. He did this to establish new customers to replace those he lost through death or cancellation.

Insurance salesman Dale Y. retired at age 35 with a financial worth of $1,000,000.

UNCOVERING MANY SELDOM KNOWN FIELDS OF OPERATION

There is the hustler-type salesman who makes a killing on a current trend, and then when the bubble bursts, moves to something else with equal appeal.

One such trend was records which played during a person's sleeping hours, pouring information to the subconscious mind. There have been records of this kind which taught foreign languages, relaxation, improved health conditions and numerous other things. There have been special amusement gadgets for children and young adults that took the country by storm for several months at a time and special exercise machines to take the place of jogging, to name but a few.

For the enterprising salesman with special abilities in anticipating coming trends this is a way to make several thousand—sometimes several million—dollars fast. It is a risky area, as are most quick-money opportunities, because it is not easy to second-guess the general public and what trends it will follow.

RETIRED MAN MAKES HALF A MILLION IN REAL ESTATE

Sam M. had worked 22 years for a plumbing and electrical supply shop as a clerk when he was fired for his refusal to work Sundays. For the next few years he eked out a living buying and selling plumbing and electrical supplies he purchased at auctions and sold to supply houses at bargain prices.

All this changed when, at 67 years of age, he sold his brother on investing in a piece of property in which Sam saw great potential. He, his brother and their father developed this land into a small subdivision, building just a few houses at a time. They sold these and built more with the profits. In a short time the business boomed. At age 71, Sam was worth a half million dollars and was still going strong.

All his life he never made more than $60 a week on which he supported five children; now he is worth more than any of his children, all of whom are in top professional positions. Sam could live off his real estate earnings for the rest of his days, but he's having too much fun making money.

HOSPITALIZATION PROFITABLE SIDELINE
FOR GENERAL AGENT

Floyd Byrns, general agent for a large casualty insurance company, recognized a need for hospitalization among a group of agents associated with the largest casualty company in the west. He recognized this as a line of business they should be writing and communicated his idea to some of the company's top agents. After three special meetings, other agents were invited to a final meeting at which all of them contributed a sum of $41,000–$1,500 apiece. Then they set up a corporation, made application and received the necessary permits from the state. They raised additional money through a stock issue and became an operating company.

Floyd was elected president; he has remained in this post for the past six years. This sideline business is bringing him $3,000 additional income per month for approximately 20 hours a week of his time. He sees a potential here within the near future for $150,000 a year.

CAPITALIZING ON BIG DEMAND FOR COSTUME JEWELRY

Cecelia V. was a factory worker earning less than $100 a week when she was invited to a jewelry party at a neighbor's home. She was so impressed with the quality of the jewelry, the profits made in only two hours and the realization that this business required no initial investment of any kind that she became a distributor immediately. From the start Cecelia made more in a week from her part-time jewelry sales than she ever did on her regular job.

In less than a year she became a unit director with others working under her. She then decided to give up her factory job and make the jewelry line her career. Cecelia was selected branch manager of the company's sales forces throughout the state. From here she moved into the position of regional manager. She now supervises more than 500 salespeople. Her income is between $40,000 and $50,000 a year.

GOOD MONEY IN FOOD AND SPICES

Grant S. was taking home about $100 a week working as a grocery clerk when someone told him about a direct selling program for food and other household products. He discovered that this company, through its door-to-door salespeople, sold extracts, spices, vitamins, cosmetics, animal feed supplements, medicines, insecticides and household aids. The investment required was less than $50. Grant started working for the company as a sideline to his grocery store job. In a short time his sales increased to considerably more than his salary. He eventually quit the store and went into the sales work full time.

Through the sales plan he built a group of distributors under him and, within a couple of years, was making as much as $3,000 a month working only 10 to 12 hours a week.

SELLING BETTER HEALTH FOR BIG PROFITS

Martha P. was a farmer's wife who wanted only enough money to put central heating in their house and a carpet on the floor.

When she heard of a program for selling food supplements that required an investment of only $60 she decided to try it. It was her plan to work it only long enough to acquire these two things.

Martha discovered very early in her new project that good food supplements were wanted and needed by a lot of people and that there was a real satisfaction in selling them. Consequently, she continued selling until she could afford not only a central heating plant and a carpet but a whole new house and more.

Martha began to reinvest her earnings in the business and borrow from other sources for additional capital until she developed a sizeable group of distributors working under her. Her real chance came when she discovered a religious sect that wanted to make more money for the expansion of their business and their daily living. She began enlisting these people all over the United States, Hawaii and Australia, holding sales meetings wherever she went. This opened a whole new and exciting life of travel to her, and her earnings soon grew to $50,000 a year and more.

HOUSEWIFE MAKES TOP MONEY SELLING ENCYCLOPEDIA

Grace B. was a school teacher who needed money during the summer months to send her son and daughter to camp and to pay her own household expenses. To get this she started working part time in encyclopedia sales, expecting to return to her teaching job in the fall. Grace was so successful in her part-time work she decided to do it as a full-time occupation. She made as much as $600 a month part time, enjoying every minute of it.

She liked the work because she was doing more than earning a good living—she was helping people as well.

It was not a difficult profession to develop because the company advertised extensively on a national basis and distributed leads to its sales people. There was also an opportunity to develop special promotional projects which could triple and quadruple sales. Often Grace would go into a business or professional complex and make a presentation. To groups such as this the encyclopedia company gave generous discounts, making it possible for the sales person to make a more attractive offer. These promotions developed volume sales and had much to do with the large amount of business Grace was able to produce.

Her initial investment was only $30 and her full-time income grew to as much as $2,000 a month.

BIG BUSINESS IN HOME PRODUCT SALES

In their 20 years of marriage before he found the opportunity to sell a nationally-known home product line, Jay C. worked at two jobs and sometimes three to provide for his wife and children. His principal job was with a weekly newspaper and job printing plant. When that business collapsed, he found himself out of a job with few prospects. When all his savings were gone and things looked pretty desperate he was introduced to a home products program. It offered an opportunity for both Jay and his wife Lisa to sell the products directly to retail customers and also to enlist other salespeople to work under them.

For a time, after their business prospered, they became complacent and merely sat back and enjoyed the fruits of their labors. Soon they discovered it was necessary for them to continue their own efforts, to some degree, along with those of their salespeople.

As time went on, their whole family became part of the business—sons, daughters, and their wives and husbands.

Their initial investment was only $34. The business is now earning for them $4,000 or more a month.

A SELDOM-USED METHOD
FOR SELLING TV ADVERTISING SPACE

Pete C. was a young advertising salesman who worked for a couple of years in a large agency until he established himself in the community. He then opened an agency of his own. To meet the competition and develop more accounts, he found it necessary to come up with some innovative ideas. Most of the big accounts in the community were already clients of the established agencies, so he decided to concentrate on some of the smaller low-budget accounts and build a business clientele from this.

He explored the cost of time on the one local TV station that was not on any of the networks; then he approached various groups of businesses for a combined advertising plan. He was able to purchase 15 minutes of TV morning time for each group at a total cost of less than $100. He started working with some of the smaller shopping centers and branched out to sections in the city where a number of different businesses were located in close proximity to each other. Pete studied the businesses he wished to approach then laid out a plan for advertising several of these businesses in one 15-minute block. He called the block the "Bargain Spot." Each one of his advertisers featured on it a lead bargain item or service for the day. It was sort of a TV classified ad featuring spectacular bargains.

He was able to get as many as 10 advertisers in one 15-minute block, so the cost to each individual advertiser was minimal. It had appeal to TV viewers because the bargains offered were good ones, and the viewing audience—particularly the women—watched for this spot regularly to see what bargains were being offered each day.

He was able to sell his idea to six shopping centers and several other business clusters. Each business gave him an advance payment which covered the cost of artwork and paid for the station time. This special project alone brought Pete as much as $1,500 additional income for his new agency every month.

BIG VOLUME IN DOOR-TO-DOOR SALES
OF WOMEN'S FASHIONS

Beeline Fashions was started by a World War II veteran and his wife with a $2,000 GI loan and their savings. They sold clothing door to door and in some cases, through the party plan.

This man and his wife started the business in a small office furnished only with a beat-up typewriter, a desk and makeshift shelves nailed to the walls. They began with eleven items of apparel and advertised these with a one-page mimeographed sheet. Over a period of some twenty years their operation expanded to $5,000,000 annual business, filling half a million orders of approximately $10 each.

There are a number of clothing manufacturers selling their merchandise by this method with some of their salespeople using the party plan extensively. It can be a profitable enterprise for a woman with many contacts, especially among friends who work and who need to dress well on a budget.

SHY YOUNG HOUSEWIFE BECOMES TOP SALES PERSON

Jewel J. needed extra money so she and her family could move from their tiny four-room cottage to more adequate quarters, and she enrolled in a sales training course in hopes of improving her earning power.

During one of the class periods, when students were demonstrating their sales presentations, some of the other girls giggled at Jewel's timid presentation. One of them said sarcastically, "What ever made you think you could learn to sell, Jewel?"

That was all it took to start this shy young lady on the road to success; she determined then to show everyone in that room that she could sell. She went out into the field immediately and started selling cut glass tableware. By the end of the first week she had the highest sales in the entire group.

Later her husband joined her in the business. Together they sold as much as $30,000 worth of cut glass in a week.

PROFITABLE TRAVELING FOR THE PERSON WHO SELLS

Any of the sales programs which use the pyramid method of distributorship offer excellent opportunities for profitable traveling. Some of the biggest money-earners in the field have distributors in their chains operating for all sections of the country. It is impossible to build a strong organization throughout the country without personal visits from the sponsor. The direct distributor who wants to make big money needs to travel. He or she needs to make that traveling pay off by setting up new sales forces wherever the traveling is done.

There are many other areas for traveling sales work that are also highly profitable. I traveled three states a few years ago selling wholesale gift merchandise. My traveling companion and I purchased a trailer which served as a mobile display room for my gift items and her stationery and greeting cards. The trailer eliminated the need for hotel displays and carrying heavy sample cases in small towns. We worked hard, but we saw a lot of interesting country in Arizona, New Mexico and southern California. Our investment was about $3,000 between us for the small aluminum trailer. We didn't have to purchase the merchandise since we took orders from samples. It is possible to make $1,000 a month or more in this type of sales work.

NUMEROUS PRODUCTS TO CHOOSE FROM

As the wide variety of sales stories in this chapter indicate, there are all kinds of sales opportunities and products to sell. If selling is your field, you should have no trouble finding the particular item or service with which you can earn the most. There are openings for big-paying sales positions in insurance, real estate, jewelry, home products, cosmetics, health aids and an endless number of other items or intangibles.

This chapter contains only a few, so don't let it limit you.

Whatever type of selling you excel in, look for that kind of opportunity. I'm sure you will find it if you look hard enough and your desire and determination are strong enough. It's a great field and the money potential is limitless.

14

Building Toward a
Full-Time Business
or Retirement

Second-income businesses frequently lead into full-time highly successful operations. The secret to this lies in the fact that second-income businesses can be developed without financial stress and strain. You can sustain yourself adequately from your full-time occupation while you develop a business operation on the side. This means you can move ahead gradually, developing good business procedures without the concerns or worries of having enough money to pay for groceries and rent.

Developing a sideline business while you are still working at another occupation also gives you the opportunity to select the type of work you most enjoy doing. When you discover a way to make good money doing what you like to do, you have uncovered the next big secret to a successful business operation. It is much easier to do whatever is necessary to succeed in a business when all the hours you spend at that business are pleasant as well as profitable.

DOING THINGS YOUR OWN WAY

One of the biggest advantages in operating your own business is the fact that there are no limitations on your efforts because of a need to operate on someone else's ideas. In your own business you can follow your creative instincts and arrange your hours for operation. The sky is the limit for development and growth.

FASHION MODEL DEVELOPS SUCCESSFUL
CONVENTION PROGRAMS

Fashion model Nancy Pavlik discovered these advantages when she branched out from modeling to a business of her own offering special programs to wives at conventions. While modeling for guests at an Arizona resort hotel she discovered a secret ability which made her more popular. She had a talent for public speaking enjoyed by few models.

"Fashion models are plentiful," Nancy said, "but models who are good commentators are more difficult to find."

MORE OPPORTUNITIES OPEN

From her success here she received offers to speak at conventions. She developed special regional presentations speaking on such things as silver jewelry, Indian life and other subjects.

The secret of Nancy's successful shows was her unique approach—entirely different from the usual presentation. She emphasized the western motif—clothes especially geared to that part of the country, such as cowboy leathers, Indian fabrics, western jewelry and fashions from Mexico.

When convention planners began to ask for other things in addition to these shows, she started taking convention wives on special tours.

There was no investment involved in the fashion shows, but the tours required an investment of about $1,800 for brochures, the services of an artist, letterheads and record books. An additional investment of about $2,000 for office equipment was also necessary. At the height of the season it is easy to make as much as $5,000 to $6,000 a month in this type of work.

IDEAL HOURS FOR WORKING MOTHER

Nancy, the mother of five children, finds this a perfect situation for her. She works only five hours a day—from 9:30 a.m. to 3:30 p.m.—and is able to prepare breakfast for her family before going to work, and arrive home before they do in the afternoon. Sometimes Nancy works ten days in a row, sometimes maybe only one day a week.

FIVE WAYS TO ESTABLISH A BUSINESS
WITH MINIMUM RISK

1. *Choose a business in which you are knowledgeable.*

The secret to any successful business operation is knowledge. The more you know about a business the more certain you are of success. Before you invest any amount of time or money in a venture you should discover all you can about that operation. If you have not had experience in the field, study everything you can about it from books, periodicals or schools.

In many cases, there are opportunities to work for someone else temporarily until you learn the basics of a particular operation, but the ideal situation is a business of your own based on your own background of experience.

EXPERT TURNS KNOWLEDGE INTO PROFITS

Jules P. worked installing photographic equipment for a large international firm. He decided, after several years of this experience, to open his own plant. Jules didn't have a college education but learned the necessary techniques through correspondence schools and was highly successful in this field before going into the business on his own.

When he was ready for retirement at 65, he borrowed close to $90,000 with which to build a 35,000 square-foot plant for the production of photo finishing equipment. Seven years later the plant had expanded to 80,000 square feet and was grossing over a quarter of a million dollars annually.

2. *Locate where the demand is the greatest.*

Some areas are better suited to certain types of businesses than others. One of the secrets of good marketing is discovering the right location for your particular business. If your product or service has strong appeal for older people, a location where many senior citizens live would be the most profitable. On the other hand, if you can sell more easily to students, a location near a school is ideal.

A GOOD EXAMPLE

The Small Business Administration makes available to prospective businesses a variety of pamphlets on specialized businesses.

The SBA's *Small Business Bibliography No. 42* discusses bookstore operations in detail. One strong emphasis in this pamphlet is the importance of proper location. It states: "The location of the bookstore is of prime importance. One of the factors to be considered is the sales potential. It has been suggested that bookstores—to be successful—must have a sales potential of at least $50,000 a year, and preferably $100,000.

"If possible, the new store should be in an area not already being serviced or where competition is not too great. Bookstores on or near college campuses are more likely to be successful. A downtown location is the best second choice. Heavy traffic areas are important since book buying is mostly impulse. Many people passing a bookstore will come into the store to browse. Browsing sells more books than any other kind of merchandising. It should be encouraged. The store itself should be spacious enough to allow self-selection service."

The SBA says the actual amount of investment for such an operation will vary according to size, but that capital should be determined with a safety margin. Figure all costs of operation in advance. With enough capital to cover these initial expenses and with the proper location, bookstore operations have proven to be a very successful businesses.

3. *Turn a profitable hobby into a business venture.*

If you now have a hobby which has been profitable, even on a small scale, it is already a proven operation with very little risk involved in the development of a larger full-time business venture.

The secret here is not to change any of your operational activities which proved successful in the small-scale program. If you were selling your product successfully on a small scale, you were operating in a position of power in that situation. Continue doing those same things in your expanded business.

HOUSEWIFE DEVELOPS HOBBY INTO PROFITABLE BUSINESS

Phyllis Huhn, a housewife and part-time artist, started an artists' supply business as a hobby when she had no real need to earn extra money. Her situation then changed abruptly, making it essential that she put all her efforts into making it a totally profitable operation.

She invested $7,000 in the business from her own cash resources but had sources available for financing if she needed it. She bought out another shop and purchased brushes, books, canvas, wood, prints, varnish and all kinds of paint—a full line of art supplies.

There were no oil paintings in the original shop but Phyllis started immediately displaying the works of various artists in oils, along with her own, until her shop became a successful art gallery as well as artists' supply house. She also added classes in oil and china painting. In two and a half years Decorative Arts and Gallery has tripled its inventory and takes in as much as $3,000 in a month. The secret to her success was the proper utilization of an already successful hobby.

4. *Meet a demand where competition is minimal.*

Wherever there is an unfilled need for a product or service, success is reasonably assured for the person who can fill that need satisfactorily. The secrets of success in a venture of this nature are discovering where such needs exist and fulfilling them effectively.

This can be accomplished through survey, as described earlier in this book, and matching the needs to your abilities.

SUCCESSFUL BUSINESS STARTED IN REMOTE COMMUNITY

Sam P. and his wife Rose followed this procedure when they started a department store and service station in a remote mining community where no such businesses existed. They borrowed $25,000 from the Small Business Administration for equipment, inventory and working capital.

In approximately seven years the business grossed over $2 million, seven times its gross the first year in business.

5. *Sell a popular product.*

There are some products for which the supply seldom surpasses the demand. The secret to successful product merchandising is finding and promoting products which continue in popularity over the years. You can do this by first listing the types of businesses best suited to your capabilities, then making a study of some of these operations in your area. Visit those which appeal the most to you and see how many customers they seem to serve from day to day. Then select your own operation accordingly.

The Small Business Administration, in their pamphlet, *Small Business Bibliography No. 76,* indicates that pet shops have in recent years become a specialized billion-dollar industry.

The pamphlet states that, according to a national report, dogs account for 40 percent of all pets sold annually. Fish sales, the report says, cover approximately 25 percent of the market, and nearly 8 million families in the U.S. own birds.

The SBA pamphlet says a business such as this can be started with from $15,000 to $35,000, and that owners of such shops earn from $10,000 to $25,000 a year.

If this business interests you, check with the SBA for possible financing.

PUTTING YOUR EXPERIENCE TO GOOD WORK

Whether you are interested in developing a full-time business operation of your own in the early years of your life or you are making plans for retirement, the secrets to success are the same. Wherever possible, put your own past experience to work for you. The man who is nearing retirement age probably has the greatest advantage here, because he has usually accumulated a good many years of experience from which to draw.

HIGHWAY ENGINEER DEVELOPS SUCCESSFUL CONSTRUCTION COMPANY

Zack J. worked for a number of years as a highway engineer in the eastern part of the United States. Upon retirement he decided to put this experience to work for him.

He started his own construction company with $15,000, half of which he was able to borrow. His first year of business produced $100,000 in sales. Twelve years later that figure was increased to $8,000,000.

Zack says the secret to his success can be attributed to his know-how plus a lot of perseverance, good workmanship and excellent employee relations.

BUSINESSMAN REVEALS SECRETS TO HIS SUCCESS

Charles Engels was a hairdresser working in someone else's shop. He wanted to start his own shop but needed $10,000 to do this, so he started doing a lot of odd jobs on the side. He sold vacuum cleaners and encyclopedias evenings. He also painted house numbers on curbs. He held all these jobs within this same period of time—doing whichever one was feasible at the moment—never wasting any of his spare time.

After accumulating the money and purchasing a beauty shop he ran this successfully for eight years. He then sold it to his employees, who are operating it with equal success.

With the money acquired from the sale of his beauty shop, he opened a cheese shop in another state.

INNOVATIONS PRODUCE PROFITABLE BUSINESS

There were other cheese shops in the area, but Engels made his business unique. He brought in perishable French cheeses which had never been available in the area before, and carried a greater variety of cheese than anyone else in the state. Within a six-year period he was operating five retail cheese shops, one restaurant and a wholesale cheese-cracker-meat business throughout the state. His net income is about $40,000 a year and would be considerably more if he were not putting many times more than that amount back into the growth of his business. Soon he plans to enter direct-mail sales as well.

The total cost for starting this business was $35,000. He had to buy a walk-in refrigerator, reach-in refrigerator, delicatessen case, scales, cash register, counter, shelves, display tables and between $8,000 and $10,000 worth of inventory.

Engels says the secrets to his success are the willingness to work 80 hours a week when necessary to get going and the courage to act without analyzing at times and correct whatever errors may result from this. He says it is essential that an executive be willing to do any job—that he never feel a task is beneath his dignity.

TEN SECRETS FOR A SUCCESSFUL BUSINESS OPERATION

1. Find out what is in demand and supply it.
2. Make sure you also give service if you sell something of value.
3. Always keep your word no matter how difficult it is.
4. Allow total reasonableness while explaining something to an employee; then, if he doesn't handle things properly, be unreasonable.
5. Your product must be as represented.

6. Satisfy the customers you already have first before seeking new ones.

7. Give speedy service. Charles Engels has a picture of a frog on his delivery truck with a sign which reads: "You crawl. We leap."

8. If someone has a complaint, handle it; but don't waste endless time with the chronic complainer thereby neglecting some of your good customers.

9. Every successful business needs the services of a good lawyer, accountant and banker.

10. Even when a professional accountant is employed, every business person should take at least one course in accounting to learn the important basics of business procedure.

SHARING YOUR PROFITS IS GOOD BUSINESS

Sometimes a person goes into business for himself because he wants all the profits. According to Charles Engels this doesn't work. He says the real secret to making money is sharing it with others who help you make it. Exist to give service more than to make money, he says, and share your profits with your employees. He makes sure everyone who works for him experiences gains whenever he does. "It's a hard and fast rule," Engel says, "that you get more by giving some away."

Some of the most successful companies in the country discovered this years ago when they initiated profit sharing for employees. Today many companies have this plan.

TOOLS SALESMAN TURNS NEEDED SERVICE
INTO SUCCESSFUL BUSINESS

Orville Valleskey was a representative for a snap-on tool company when he decided to open a tool rental and small machinery operation, a much-needed service where he lived.

With approximately $24,000, half of which he borrowed through the Small Business Administration, he purchased small tractors, land tillers, cement mixers and small contractors' and gardening equipment. In nine years his business grew from $30,000 gross with no employees to $300,000 gross and 11 employees.

He saw a need and filled it—that was the secret of his success.

WORKING AT WHAT YOU REALLY LIKE

So many hours of every day are spent earning a living it is important to work at what you like. Second-income occupations often open the door which eventually leads to a full-time business doing what you really like to do.

ARTIST'S PAINTINGS FINANCE BUSINESS OF HIS CHOICE

This was the case with artist John R. Thompson. He was national advertising director for the U.S. Plywood Corporation which is now part of Champion International. Later he took charge of national advertising for the Weyerhauser Corporation. During this period he was painting on the side—doing oils, water colors and drawings which he would show and sell. Two of his drawings, in fact, are part of the famous Peggy Guggenheim collection in Venice.

Over a period of time he built his artwork sales to the point where he could start his own gallery. Thompson bought out a framing business for an investment of $38,000, financing all but $10,000 which was paid for through the sale of his artwork.

When he took over this business he had to purchase framing equipment, moldings and ready-made frames. He started a gallery immediately, taking all the artwork on consignment. In his gallery he handles all kinds of painting, sculpture, drawings and graphics. In a short three years Thompson built his business to a $10,000 monthly gross income.

One of his success secrets is the consistency with which he continued developing the sales of his own artwork while continuing a full-time occupation. He advises also, for a less risky operation, that you buy a successfully operating business, as he did, and be sure to hire salespeople who do not antagonize your customers.

SELF-EMPLOYMENT ADVANTAGES AFTER RETIREMENT

Many active people find retirement a rather dull experience and are eager to find something to occupy their time. Some of the happiest retirees are those who have come out of retirement and gone into a productive business operation. This is a time when you can be selective about your means of earning a living, and you can choose a business that suits not only your experience but your interests as well.

MOST SUCCESSFUL BUSINESS STARTED AFTER RETIREMENT

Ralph Kassing was a retired district representative for General Electric who came out of retirement after 11 months because he couldn't stand doing nothing. He went into a store to buy some envelopes and noted the store's rundown condition. What they needed, he concluded, was either more merchandise or someone to share their space with them. He made an agreement with the owner to do the latter and put General Electric appliances in his side of the building. Kassing had been a sales representative for 22 years before his retirement, selling small appliances to wholesalers. He traveled through Maryland, Virginia, Delaware and the District of Columbia before being transferred to the southeastern part of the United States.

TURNING PAST EXPERIENCE INTO BIG PROFITS

His background in this field gave him excellent qualifications for starting a business he enjoyed. It was especially rewarding to be in his own business where he had full control.

Kassing started with a $12,000 inventory and part-time book-keeper. Two years later he had an inventory of $100,000 and nine employees. Within two years he became the largest General Electric appliance dealer in the state. He then added patio furniture to his stock.

The secret to this successful operation, which brings in as much as $50,000 net annually, is a thorough knowledge of the business and a real affinity for it.

SOCIAL SECURITY BENEFITS WITH SELF-EMPLOYMENT

The maximum yearly sum a person is allowed to earn in addition to Social Security payments doesn't offer much in the way of comfortable living. This is particularly true if you work for someone else. It is possible to earn considerably more without a severe loss in Social Security payments if you are self-employed. If you earn money from your own business only part of the year, you lose your Social Security payments only for the months you are receiving more than the monthly amount allowed.

For example, if you earned $10,000 in one month from your business and nothing the rest of the year, your Social Security payments would be withheld only for that month. If you earned $25,000 in a six-month period, your Social Security payments would be withheld only during that six month period. The rest of the year you would receive full payment.

OTHER INCOMES THAT DO NOT COUNT AGAINST SOCIAL SECURITY

You do not need to count against Social Security benefits your earnings in interest, dividends or rentals from real estate (unless received by a real estate dealer or a farm landlord who materially participates in the production of farm commodities on the land rented). Pensions and insurance policy payments for disability or accident do not count against Social Security payments either, nor do royalties on patents or copyrights unless you are writing or inventing on a continuing basis.

THE SECRET TO SUCCESSFUL RETIREMENT PLANNING

This secret is summed up in a few words in an article in *Today's Health* expressing the opinions of Dr. Marc H. Hollender and Stanley A. Frankel on retirement. The essence of it is "Retire people *to* something, rather than *from* something."

There are many examples of retired people who are just beginning some of their most successful businesses. They are making more money now than ever before and having a ball in the process.

RETIRED COUPLE DEVELOPED HALF A MILLION DOLLAR BUSINESS

Kurt C. was a national sales representative for menswear when he retired and opened a small dress shop with his wife Bea. They bought a particular dress from a seamstress to sell in their store. This item was so successful that they began to produce it in quantity. A representative of a nationally-known specialty house saw the dress and asked to have some made for her own sales operation.

Kurt and Bea decided then to open a small dress factory. They bought half a dozen sewing machines, investing about $5,000 in the business. For the next ten years they specialized in this particular type dress. When they later sold the business, it was worth half a million dollars.

LITTLE KNOWN AIDS FOR
FREE GOVERNMENT ASSISTANCE

You can obtain a list of approximately 30,000 booklets, pamphlets and books by writing to the Superintendent of Documents, U.S. Government Printing Office, Washington, D.C. From this list you can select any that might help you in your search for either a business career, a job or merely a more productive approach to your retirement years.

The Small Business Administration offers extensive free help to the individual wishing to go into a small business operation. It offers a large selection of free booklets and pamphlets relating to almost any kind of business venture which might interest you. Management consultants are also available through SBA's SCORE program. There is no charge for this service. SCORE is made up of retired business professionals with specialists in a wide variety of businesses.

ENJOYING THE FRUITS OF YOUR LABORS

Whatever you do, whether you develop a full-time business of your own in the early years of your life or after retirement, make it a pleasant experience as well as a profitable one. Work can be as much fun as leisure activity if properly chosen.

The world is full of successful business people doing what they like to do. Join them in combining business with pleasure. You will live longer—and better.

Index